Ramchandra Singh's diary is a telling of its times—the naxal movement, the Emergency and repression, all crucial events that influenced life in the Seventies. It is valuable because little seems to have changed in Indian prisons. Thirteen years behind bars can very well deaden one's sensitivity but Ramchandra's honest account of fetters, love and revolution sparkles with life.
Arun Ferreira, author of *Colours of the Cage*

This is a memoir about revolution, life and love told from the heart. Its simplicity and truthfulness is immensely moving. We learn of the role of the state and the Emergency in shaping the emotional and political evolution of a humane and sensitive young man in the 1970s and 1980s. I salute him.
K.R. Meera, author of *Hangwoman*

Singh's story is a representative saga. This smuggled-out account exposes the bosom of the Gulag that India has become. A must read.
Anand Teltumbde, writer and civil rights activist

The world of the prison is not just of confinement but being shorn of all autonomy. Indian prisons are dark reflections of our society, laden as they are with deep hypocrisies. The fact that Ramchandra Singh's account retains a humane sensibility is testimony to the resilience of the human spirit. He is not just a survivor, but one who can with this diary

hold a mirror to our collective shame. If we in India want not a retributive system of justice but a reformatory one—for only through it can we in any real sense lay claim to being civilised—we urgently need to address the concerns raised by Singh's diary. A must read for those in high places.
Teesta Setalvad, author of *Foot Soldier of the Constitution: A Memoir*

Ramchandra Singh began his tryst with the people's movements in Uttar Pradesh—not a place known to be active during the Naxalbari uprising. He was part of an armed agrarian struggle encompassing the area from Unnao to the Nepal borders. Singh raises our spirits with the earthy fragrance of his 'criminal' life. His memoir, in fact, bears the fragrance of fire.
Varavara Rao, author of *Captive Imagination: Letters from Prison*

13 Years

A Naxalite's Prison Diary

Ramchandra Singh

with a foreword by Angela Davis

Translated from the Hindi by Madhu Singh

navayana

13 Years: A Naxalite's Prison Diary

First published 2018; first paperback edition February 2022

ISBN 9788195539239

First serialised in Hindi in Rashtriya Sahara, 1984; first published
by the journal Samkaleen Dastavez in Lucknow, 1991

Navayana Publishing Pvt Ltd
155 2nd Floor
Shahpur Jat, New Delhi 110049
Phone: +91-11-26494795
navayana.org

Distributed in South Asia by HarperCollins India

Subscribe to updates at navayana.org/subscribe
Follow on facebook.com/Navayana

Contents

Foreword

13 Years: My Story as a Naxalite in Prison is a stunning account of the journey one human being makes through a labyrinth of pain and repression and through the most debased dimensions of humanity, as exemplified both by his jailers and by the conditions of prison life. However, the author of this memoir also acquires insights and develops practices that rescue him from the dehumanising fate this repression is designed to produce. Ramchandra Singh's story is indeed uniquely his own, and yet it is connected to many themes that have been the hallmark of political prisoner accounts for generations. Singh's is a coming-of-age story of a revolutionary driven to move his world towards justice and equality, as well as the story of a radical activist behind bars, who begins to reflect deeply on tactics he previously embraced that, to his more mature self, seem to contravene the very goal of revolutionary struggle. It is also the story of love—romantic passion, as well as friendship and parental devotion.

Most impressively, Singh's memoir demonstrates a deep

engagement with language—captured seamlessly in Madhu Singh's translation from the Hindi—which allows him to produce heart-rending descriptions of the effects of violence on his own body, compelling speculations on the temporal distortions of imprisonment, and interesting observations about the relationship between politics and love. His evocative prose opens the door to experiences that are otherwise beyond the apprehension of those who have not had the misfortune of learning firsthand the nature of imprisonment.

Although readers in the West are familiar with the works of such political prisoners as Antonio Gramsci, Elizabeth Gurley Flynn, Nelson Mandela, George Jackson, Assata Shakur and Mumia Abu-Jamal, they are largely unaware of the circumstances that have created a significant tradition of political imprisonment in India. Given that the writings of these European, U.S. and South African figures are evoked by contemporary movements, particularly given the increasing focus on the prison industrial complex, Ramchandra Singh's book should resonate with the present.

As the world acknowledges the West's marking of 1968 as a pivotal year of protests—from the student uprising in Paris to the demonstration by athletes Tommie Smith and John Carlos in the Mexico City Olympics—so also should the Naxalbari uprising of 1967 be globally recognised. Two generations after the protests of the late sixties, young people around the world are calling for economic, racial and gender justice, for justice towards the environment as well as for immigrants and refugees. They are recognising a continuum of anti-capitalist theory and praxis from the era of Marx to the present and are studying historical socialist uprisings. Strikingly, this prison memoir represents a more contemporary period; it allows us not only to understand the continual relevance of socialist resistance, but also the problems and internal contradictions within such movements. Debates on the role of violence and armed struggle, which have a very long history, are highlighted throughout the text and will certainly help activist readers to think critically about various modes of struggle and understand the central importance of mass organising to any attempt to effect radical change.

Nelson Mandela and his comrades often referred to prison as a university—indeed former political prisoners who conduct tours to Robben Island often speak of it as Robben Island University. We are also accustomed to accounts by political prisoners of study groups, classes, meetings on subjects related to radical struggles for justice. For example, Antonio Gramsci created an educational project during his internment on the island of Ustica, which was emulated by political prisoners in other places of confinement in Italy during the period of fascist repression. While Ramchandra Singh's accounts of his involvement in a specifically political education will help the reader to understand some of the central debates within his movement, it is his encounters with ordinary prisoners (those who had not been involved in political struggle) that are especially revelatory—producing numerous insights about his own political mission, as well as understandings about the functioning of the prison, including the role of class and caste.

Abolitionist theorists and activists have acknowledged that the dynamic between political prisoners and those whose unlawful acts may not have been politically motivated has helped us to apprehend the difference between prison reform (which has had its advocates since the very invention of the prison) and prison abolition, which invites us to imagine a social system in which prisons will have become obsolete. Activists around the world should come to appreciate the way in which Ramchandra Singh imagines the possibility of a world without crime. In this world, class and caste differences would no longer determine who is and who isn't subject to state repression. Military and police forces would no longer serve as the false guarantors of security, and there would be no need for prisons and other places of confinement. This moves us in the direction of new visions of socialism.

Angela Davis
23 January 2018
University of California, Santa Cruz

I

The first days

The rivulets of blood that had trickled down my face were dry and strands of hair were plastered untidily across my bloodied forehead. How I fancied my hair once and how carefully I had kept myself groomed. The open gash that cut from the right eye across to the jaw was so grotesque that if I were a child I would have been scared to see it. Or I may have clapped and squealed with delight because I now resembled the man who played Hanuman during the Ramlila in our qasbah. So many memories of childhood flashed before my dazed, half-conscious mind and vanished.

My childhood wasn't going to come back—it never does. It seemed that my youth would begin and end within these high walls of confinement. Even if I were ever released, there would be nothing left of me. I would be a living corpse. My hair grey and my head trembling like an earthen pot perched atop thin and supple reeds of sarpat. Oscar Wilde had once said that each day in prison feels like a year, and each year like an era—this was truly the case.

I was unable to walk. My legs hurt badly, the knees were

swollen and I didn't dare rest my weight on my toes. Every cell of my body throbbed with excruciating pain. My back and arms had turned blue and were spotted with blood. Inflammation had set in along my left arm—I couldn't move it—all the way down to the fingers. The right wrist was handcuffed, swollen and badly injured, like the palm. The rope attached to one end of the handcuffs was tightly wound about my waist while the other end was held securely by police constables. I was so numb with pain that the soreness of my handcuffed wrist and the chafed skin on my waist did not add much to my physical suffering, else I would have yelled and howled.

They pushed me off the parked vehicle and I lost my balance. I couldn't have held myself steady anyway, with every pore of my body crying out for help. Before me loomed an iron gate secured with enormous, ancient looking padlocks. Sentries armed with bayonets were positioned on either side of it. Motionless and cold, they stood like corpses with living eyes. On a cue, the huge gate parted a little and I was shoved in.

Once inside, after the necessary formalities, we passed through another huge gate. Before us was a large clean courtyard with neatly trimmed flower beds displaying a variety of Indian and foreign flowers in late-September bloom. During winters, the prison officials carried out their work under the sun while in summers they were seen enjoying the crisp morning breeze. After the garden came the entrance to what was known as the circle. The inner part of the circle could be reached only after crossing a long gallery and many doors which were under strict vigilance. On all sides of the inner circle were wide open spaces. Within these stood wings of barracks occupied by sickly-looking prisoners crammed like filthy insects in a box, hardly able to move.

I was taken to this circle. A couple of burly prisoners clad in yellow uniform and red caps dragged me along. Then they dumped me in the verandah of the prison hospital which was a long hall with an earthen tiled roof. The guard on duty had a few silly questions which I answered unwillingly and with great difficulty. Meanwhile, frail-looking inmates and undertrials surrounded me. Some wanted to know about me. Some roared with laughter at their own obscene jokes. I was disgusted. But was my situation better than theirs?

One of my comrades, Kishan Lal, who had already been admitted to the hospital, came out.

"Where are the others?" I asked, though I could barely speak.

"In the barracks within the circle."

This friend of mine and other comrades had been arrested three days previously and were brought to prison the next day. I had been kept in Hardoi kotwali where more than half a dozen top officials from the investigating agency interrogated me for two days, taking breaks in between. Before I could answer one question another was flung at me. I knew they would torture me till I became incoherent and disoriented. I don't remember if they could get anything out of me.

Kishan Lal too had deep cuts and wounds on his body. He took me inside, spread a blanket on the floor between two cots and made me lie down. In the evening, a ward boy handed me a bottle of red lotion and a tube of ointment. No doctor or compounder showed up. It was a terrible night.

There are two types of admission given to the sick and infirm in prison hospitals: temporary and permanent. Permanent admission ensures a better diet—some milk and fruit—while temporary admission allows only the regular food meant for prisoners. Very often these prisoners are made to tend and water vegetable patches and flowering plants for the doctors and compounders. Unless there is a threat to his life, a seriously ill prisoner is never given permanent admission. But with a little underhand dealing and by greasing the palms of petty officials anyone can avail of permanent admission and have a pretty good time. A doctor granted me temporary admission the next morning.

After the doctor's visit, I sat in the verandah trying to swallow the watery gruel-like dalia given to the temporary patients, when the warden on morning duty suddenly stood before me. His gruff voice hit my ears: "Finish your dalia and clear up the flower beds."

Alarmed, I stopped eating and looked at him. This old man looked very strange. He had on a shabby uniform over his thin and shrivelled body. The skin hung loosely from his old bones. His face resembled that of a langur. Dark shadows lurked under huge but lifeless eyes, deep lines of wrinkles creased his long face and his aged lips frothed with saliva—all these instilled an unknown fear in me. Fear and helplessness must have showed in my eyes. But nothing in his face revealed if my condition made any difference to him.

"Hurry up," he yelled.

"Can't you see what bad shape I am in?" I whined.

"Will you get up now?" He unfastened the leather belt from his waist, which threatened me into compliance.

How I wished the earth would open up and take me in along with this cruel warden. I dragged myself over to the row of flower beds. Then I tried to hold the broom tightly and somehow tidied the patch, willing myself on. The old warden's insolent eyes followed me. My eyes were wet with tears. I remembered my dead grandparents who had loved me so much.

In a short while, two other prisoners were assigned the same job. The man who distributed the dalia had left. The leaky bucket had been placed before the dalia container while it was distributed. It now overflowed with spillage. The moment the man left, a large flock of crows alighted from nowhere and made a dash for the bucket of leftover dalia. The old warden forgot all about us and chased the crows with a stick. They flew up creating a ruckus. Meanwhile, another flock of crows landed. He now ran after them. In a flicker of an eye more crows landed and the warden chased them like crazy. Finding this funny, I had started enjoying it a little.

A few other prisoners, who stood watching from a distance, were clearly enjoying it too.

I remembered a story I had heard in my childhood. A king had two wives. He neglected the elder queen in his love for the younger one. After grabbing all his wealth, the younger queen forced the king to banish the elder queen to the forest to chase crows. Time passed, people now insulted and poked fun at her. After a while the crow-chaser queen became ugly. Happiness had disappeared from her life and she continued to chase crows like a crazy woman. As love, tenderness and charm left her, she became bitter, quarrelsome and cruel. The plight of our old warden was quite like hers.

2

Food, shit, bath, haircut, expletives and sleep

A popular saying in our region goes: Garra ka paani, chatta ki roti. The Garra's muddy water, the roti of coarse husk. Life in adversity makes one tougher, so to say. To an extent, the saying made sense here. Any detainee who arrives in prison battered and bruised recovers very fast. Yes, despite poor medical facilities, contaminated drinking water and the bad food, he gets back on his feet very soon and appears as well fed and healthy as before. But this is a deceptive recovery. It doesn't last. After a while, he begins to turn gaunt and shrunken.

I felt better after washing my wounds with the red-yellow lotion, applying layers of ointment on my inflamed limbs and sunning myself. This little relief was enough to get me thrown out of hospital. Although my hands and left arm were still inflamed, they could move a little now. So I was discharged and sent to the circle.

Next, I was issued a coarse mat, three blankets, a brass plate, and a bowl. The plate and bowl had holes which had been fixed with tar. Carrying the mat and the blankets under my arm and clutching the plate and bowl, when I entered the circle, a horde of prisoners swarmed around me like flies. They were the undertrials. Many of them had heavy iron fetters on their ankles. They jangled them to prove their superior status and tried to browbeat others. Arrested when? On what grounds? From which place?—many such queries were thrust in my face.

I was very weak. I had tied around me a lungi made from the folded layers of my dirty, torn dhoti. My shirt was in tatters. A thick layer of grime covered my body. My hair was unkempt and greasy, and my feet bare. Everyone stared as if I were a strange and loathsome creature. As I stood there, dazed, I heard the call to file in for bread parade. The inmates who had surrounded me bolted in that direction, carrying their plates and bowls. Huge pots of lentils, vessels of vegetable curry and trays of chapattis arrived. The prisoners quickly fell into queue and waited their turn to be served. Then, they dispersed across the compound to eat. Several moved with their plates to their barracks.

I was ravenous. Hunger turned me almost beastly towards food. I snatched some chapattis. In my hurry to take the lentils, a little spilt on the ground. The man serving it—called the daliha since his office consists of pouring the dal—glared at me and shot off some filthy abuse which hardly affected me, occupied as I was with helping myself to the food. I went over to one side of the ground and had my fill, having hardly eaten since the previous week. Sometimes I had swallowed a little dalia, at other times a few pieces of chapatti soaked in watery dal. The meal now gave me great satisfaction though it was hardly edible. The chapattis were thin and undercooked, the dal was watery. But yes, plenty of cooked vegetable was served. Green pumpkins had been chopped into big pieces without peeling the skin, then boiled and mashed. I finished all the chapattis, dal and the remaining vegetable. I felt contented. Then I took my plate and bowl to wash. It was crowded near the tap and the inmates were busy quarrelling or jostling each other. I waited patiently amid the cacophony for quite a while. After great effort when I managed to procure a plateful of water to drink, my chest swelled up with the jubilance of a victorious soldier.

By evening, all of us were sent back into the barracks. Five to six convict-supervisors and convict-watchmen were also locked up. After the lock-up, an assistant jailor inspected us. Inside the barracks, the overseers made a headcount of the inmates in pairs and then announced at the top of their voice towards the bolted gate: "Padlocks, Windows, Lanterns—All ok—Inmates locked up. Barrack number…."

There were some eighty concrete berths in each barrack while the inmates were around one hundred and fifty. Those with berths allotted to them crept into their beds. Many squeezed into the little space between two berths and slept. Those who couldn't find even this space had to make do by spreading their folded blankets in the narrow aisle between the rows of berths. With the roll of blanket and mat secure under my arm, I watched the activities of the strange creatures of this museum. Then an inmate called out from his berth: "Put down your bedroll, go to the room with the barred window at the end of the barrack and pay your respect at the Devi's shrine. Everyone who arrives here has to pay obeisance." I looked at him a moment to figure out what exactly he meant when he growled: "What are you staring at? Go and touch the Devi's feet." Realising that he was bullying me, I told him politely, "I am too filthy right now to touch anything holy. Anyway, thanks a lot for your kind suggestion."

The moment I had finished speaking, a poor and shabby-looking inmate reprimanded him: "Get a sense of the person before you speak to him." He then held my hand and said, "Come here, I'll find you a place." This shabbily dressed inmate was Moolchand. He removed an earthen pot filled with water to accommodate me near his berth. The inmate who had earlier asked me to visit the shrine now looked small before Moolchand's generosity. He grinned sheepishly. Without asking any questions I had discovered that the shrine was nothing but the shit pot meant for the prisoners. From then on Moolchand became my close friend. Loyalty and selflessness were his hallmark. I took to calling him Comrade Moolchand and he later came to be known as Comrade by the other inmates too.

The prisoners raised a rumpus through the night. They joked, yelled, cursed, banged on their plates and sang boisterously. Undoubtedly, some of them were good singers. But at the slightest provocation they would mouth such obscenities as were simply unimaginable outside. This was perhaps their way of defying society, as they gleefully challenged and demolished the bounds of societal norms, morality and restraint. In its sting, lethality and brazenness, the prison lexicon is a thing apart from the ordinary run of bad language. After the nightly lock-up come the hours of easy talk. A desultory banter begins among the rows of occupied cement berths and continues well into the night. Should somebody break wind audibly, a voice will ring out, "Hey, stop it! Stop doing him! I've banged tighter ones than that"—and everyone bursts out laughing. Or, if a prisoner calls out to another asking if he might borrow a beedi, gur, spices, onions or anything, he will receive the answer: "Sure, just shave that chakkar (arsehole) of yours and bring it here." Such bare-faced allusions to homosexuality can cow a new prisoner encountering them for the first time.

That night, I wandered the labyrinths of my mind and though I tried my best to catch a bit of sleep, after every ten or fifteen minutes a series of patrolling and counting sounds disrupted it. All through, the night-watchmen rapped at the barred windows of the barracks with iron rods to ensure that security was not breached. At times, when the loud calls of the watchmen from all the barracks and of the sentries who tapped on the windows and of convict-watchmen at the main boundary reporting 'all-ok', sounded together, the surrounding town must have shivered with a nameless apprehension. Quite often an official or the head warden would turn up at this unearthly hour to enquire the name, number and berth of one prisoner or another. The entire experience was something new, horrifying and utterly unimagined, but later became an inseparable part of my life in prison.

The morning began with the counting of the inmates followed by prayers. After collecting a handful of boiled black gram for breakfast, when I visited the toilet in the courtyard outside the barrack, its filthy condition made me want to puke. Pots overflowed with excreta, doors were broken. Many occupants defecated standing on their toes to avoid getting defiled by the filth around; some waited their turn, while others, unable to bear the pressure, relieved themselves in the nearby drain. Things looked tough. I returned with my container of water, planning to go only when the place was cleaner.

The earthen floor of the courtyard was being mopped. An inmate had tied a piece of old blanket to a rod and dragged it about the floor while other inmates poured water on it from the nearby tank. I thought, given that there is an acute shortage of water, why clean the courtyard every day? Until the tank slowly filled up, no inmate was allowed to take a drop of water for his personal use even if his throat was parched or he needed water for ablutions or had defecated in his pajama. I too poured water on the rag like the other inmates in the bitter morning cold.

When I went to the toilet again after an hour or so, I found it clean. Placing the pot of water on the wall, I was about to relieve myself when a sweeper barged in. Perhaps he had us under watch. He carried a pair of tall and thick bamboo baskets attached to a pole, for the removal of excreta. Flapping them on the floor he yelled at me: "Out, out, out fast! Don't you dare shit now." Startled out of my wits, I got up. I could make no sense of what this new trouble was. He growled again: "You, motherfucker! The sahib hasn't taken the round as yet and here you have come to dirty it."

I understood that whatever takes place here is only to please the sahib (the superintendent). The toilet is cleaned because once in a while the bada sahib may inspect it, which the inmates call 'sniffing the pot'. Similarly, the courtyard is cleaned every day without fail despite the water shortage so that the sahib is not annoyed. But the sahib had never cared to discover the shortage of drinking water.

I moved away. At one end of the courtyard, a barber was trimming the hair of a fellow prisoner. Behind him waited a dozen more. I too fell in line. I thought of having a bath after the haircut. After a long wait, when my turn came, the barber refused to cut my hair saying that the jail rules do not permit trimming. Instead the head would be shaved. I told him that I had seen him trim the hair of an inmate a little while back. Another inmate who sat close by asked, "Do you have a bundle of beedis?" I didn't have any. How was I to procure a bundle of beedis which could have then purchased a haircut? With his machine, he shaved my head. Despite my request to be careful with the scabs on my scalp, he paid no heed.

After the bada sahib made his rounds, finding a convenient moment I went to relieve myself. Then with the little dirty water left in the tank, I somehow managed to bathe, changed into dry clothes and stood in the sun. I felt like a human being again. Moolchand poured a little oil in the cup of my hand which I applied to my face and scalp. And despite my stopping him, he ran away with my soiled clothes to wash them in the other barrack.

This is how my everyday life picked up. Within a few days I became friendly with many other inmates. I started liking those whom I had once loathed. Even their obscene talk and crass behaviour, enough to make my head ache, now appeared normal. Among prisoners outrageous language is not extraordinary at all, but a reliable fallback for amusement. For instance, if a prisoner makes tall claims or swaggers around, another will retort: "Yes Bhai, as the IG sahib's testicle you would be in the thick of things." Or, someone else's boasts might be deflated with the words, "Don't go playing the great landukhanjar (dagger-dick)—come off it!" Should a smooth-faced youngster speak of getting himself transferred to another barrack, he hears the response, "You're fine here. Over there, your arse will be turned into a cunt." This phrase was a popular and handy one, its image of transmutation applied to a variety of daily experience. Indeed, words for the anus became metaphors for every aspect of daily life in jail—with a versatility to rival the most inventive wordsmith or linguist.

Such an atmosphere was typical of the district prisons, where the undertrials predominated, and I was stuck with it for the over two years I spent at the Hardoi jail. Ultimately, the tone of these exchanges registered with me only in making me laugh, but my fellow political prisoners and I kept a non-committal distance from the raillery, saying nothing to encourage or prolong it. We were preoccupied with our own aims and ideals, and these goings on made no more than a passing impression. Nor did we try to deliver prudish sermons or censure those around us.

Among them were many who had committed heinous crimes. A few were notorious and hardened criminals. People trembled on hearing their names. But they, too, appeared normal to me. Besides Moolchand, another inmate at the Hardoi jail, Jaswant Singh, became close to me and we forged a great friendship. Born into a family of feudal thakurs, he came of middle-class peasant stock from the village of Sumerpur in Hardoi district. Jaswant had little formal education. However, seen against the traditional feudal values of his upbringing, he was a sensitive, modern young man with a quick and intense grasp of ideas. He was of average height. A clear complexion, slim body, and faint moustache added to his distinct charm. His reserved, balanced and clear-headed mien gave him a certain dignity among the other prisoners. These qualities and his sensitivity created an emotional connect and close friendship between us.

When Jaswant told me his story, I realised that each prisoner taken at face value is a criminal, but behind the jail life of each one lurks another, sadder tale. Jaswant told me that before being arrested in his village, he was in Madhya Pradesh. His family had sent him there on a task, to prevent his getting too involved with a girl back home. Jaswant had fallen in love with a thakur girl, Lakshmi, who lived next door. The roofs of their houses touched. This enabled them to meet once in a while. Gradually, not only did their families come to know of the affair but there were whispers about them in the whole village. Lakshmi's family approached Jaswant's regarding this matter but the matchmaking could proceed no further as Jaswant's family had a higher status in the area. Her family being no match for his, their marriage did not receive consent. But Jaswant's family advised the girl's parents that they should get her married off and promised that he would be kept out of the way, sent to a faraway place on the pretext of work.

While in Madhya Pradesh, Jaswant became entangled in a big looting incident. Whilst being transferred in handcuffs from one place to another, he managed to escape from the police jeep into the hills. He got his handcuffs off, and sleeping rough or finding temporary refuge all the way, made it back to his native place, Hardoi in Uttar Pradesh. As an escaped convict, he continued to evade arrest. Whenever possible he would visit his home in the village secretly, and also meet

Lakshmi. The Madhya Pradesh police was in search of him, while the local police of Uttar Pradesh, which had framed him on fake charges of dacoity, was also on the lookout.

Lakshmi's family quickly found a match for her—an unsuitable one—to get her off their hands. The day the bridegroom's party was to arrive at her place, Jaswant Singh reached his home by evening and managed to meet her on the rooftop. The night of the marriage, Lakshmi's parents got whiff of Jaswant's presence in the village. Fearing a disturbance, they informed the local police station.

Before daybreak, Jaswant went out in the fields to relieve himself. He had planned to leave the village after his morning ablutions but as he was returning from the fields, cleaning his teeth with a neem twig, he was nabbed by a large police contingent. They brought him home, beating him brutally with lathis all the way. The whole village sank into fear at his howls and cries.

When the bride Lakshmi heard his howls, she broke all barriers, rushed out in her bridal finery and embraced Jaswant amid the shower of police batons. She cried, "Please don't beat him. He has done no harm to anyone." The police batons stopped. The whole village, every man and woman, was stunned. This was unimaginable for the baratis. And even for the policemen. The inspector discreetly separated Jaswant and Lakshmi, and handed over Lakshmi to the women who had come running after her.

The police then dragged Jaswant away. As Lakshmi tried

to break free and follow him, her yellow chunar fell to the ground. She howled and her bridal makeup ran with tears. Family members held her back. She covered her face with hennaed hands and the rays of the sun caught her bright red bangles. Then she lost consciousness, and only the outstretched arms of people kept her from falling to the ground.

This was Jaswant's story. He sat before me. There were actual charges of looting against him in Madhya Pradesh, and also of escaping from police custody. Besides, the Hardoi police had falsely implicated him in a number of dacoity cases. He was now a notorious dacoit. "What will you do when you are released?" I asked. For a moment he went deep into his thoughts and then smiled and replied simply, "Loot." I couldn't understand what oceans of sorrow lay behind his gentle smile and how long an emotional journey he had made before his brief answer.

I was unable to decide who the culprit was in this complex situation. Was Jaswant solely responsible for looting or was it the result of youth's helpless addiction to a fast-living culture, needing big hauls of immediate cash, legal or illegal, to fulfill their desires and compensate for unfulfilled ones. The capitalist society and its class hierarchy ensure that lower and middle class youth search for that elusive joy of life in hotels, clubs, violence and adventure. I also wished the parents of Lakshmi and Jaswant had agreed to let them marry, but they were victims of that rigid, feudal mindset and inflated ego still common in our villages.

From Hardoi, I was sent to Unnao and later to the Fatehgarh Central Jail. I had no news of Jaswant during this period. Later, I came to know that he was released from jail, whether on bail or by court, I was unable to discover. Still later, I learned that he had been murdered.

Many of the prisoners had been framed by the police to cover up its inefficiency, instead of putting the real criminals behind bars. Among these convicts, many were poor labourers or landless peasants. These wretched people were made to clean the compound, while resourceful ones among the inmates found ways to avoid such chores. The toilers felt greatly obliged if offered a few beedis and some eatables in return. Happily, they shared the little they had received—the beedis, roasted black gram and a few balls of jaggery—with their friends. It surprised me to discover oceans of love and empathy for one another in these unkempt and poor people.

The scene during visiting hours when the inmates, seated in rows, got to meet their family members, was heartrending. When an aged father stared at his imprisoned son, eyes brimming with tears, his silence seemed to scream with agony. Wives, unable to restrain themselves, embraced their infants tightly and burst into tears as they sat beating their heads at their husbands' feet. What did all this mean? Why do such things happen?

From ancient times to the present why didn't the so-called enlightened souls—the saints and the seers, the prophets and philosophers, scholars and thinkers—formulate practical rules for our social system not to leave space for such endless misery and sorrow? This should have been the natural condition of human life evolving through the ages, that there be no killings and killers. No dacoity and no dacoits, no sign of crime. No one would be rich or poor, high or low born. We would have had no compulsion to bear the burden of a repressive state machinery, a police and an army. Prisons would not be needed at all. Such a hypothesis has been made about the communist system in which there is no class distinction. In a classless society, everyone receives a share of the production based on their needs. So, if there is no class then the government too shall not be needed. There will not be the incentive to take to crime. Actually, this hypothesis can come true only when socialism becomes successful, not in one nation alone but the entire world. In his 1924 work *Baisveen Sadi* (The Twenty-Second Century), Rahul Sankrityayan had tried to present a similar blueprint for Indian society.

How I wished the learned scholar Sankrityayan's vision for the twenty-second century could come true.

3

The trial, poetry and the farce of identification

By now, we comrades had secured a somewhat special place among the prisoners. I had two other comrades in my barrack, Amar Singh and Badri Prasad. Kishan Lal was in Barrack Number 2 in the same campus. Shivnath Trivedi, Chote Lal, Baijnath and Vibhuti Prasad were in other barracks. We were generally liked by the inmates. They knew that we had some link with politics and that there was a major political move behind charging us with the murder of a zamindar. Despite being familiar with its name, they did not know what exactly naxalism meant and how and why one becomes a naxal.

The inmates often questioned us about our mission, and we tried our best to make them understand. But many of the things we told them simply went over their heads. In answer to one of their queries when I said that our purpose was to start an armed struggle in India, one of them asked, "What does this mean?" I got irritated at their stupidity but it hit me later that they were no fools; indeed I was one. My mission was not clear even to me—revolution can only be a means but not the goal, it can be a path, not the destination.

Sometimes a bold prisoner rudely pointed out, "You have killed people, so you are also criminals. How can you call yourselves political leaders?" There was no way I could make them understand that politics was bloodless war and war was gory politics. But were we responsible for the war? Did we have our armed force? Did we ever try to build a political base among the masses? Unable to provide answers to these and many similar questions, I often became frustrated and confined within myself.

One day during parade I met the bada sahib with our demand to be shifted to the A-Class ward—since we were political prisoners—and also asked for exemption from the labour of cleaning and mopping, sleeping on the floor, and daily parades. We further demanded a better diet and reading facilities. The sahib looked me up and down, and glanced at my history-sheet. The officials with him informed him that I was a naxalite. Curtly dismissing my request, he said, "Nothing can be done. We cannot provide you with separate accommodation."

After the sahib finished his round many inmates surrounded me, curious to know what had passed. It was strange for them to see that I spoke to the sahib directly. That evening, before the barrack was locked up we did not take out our bedroll. Seeing that comrade Kishan Lal hadn't taken out his bedroll, the circle officer who came to lock our Barrack Number 1 cursed him with filthy invective. Kishan Lal couldn't take it and retaliated. The circle officer, along with a few overseers, pounced on him and thrashed him till he fainted. Later, he was sent to the hospital. The jailor had also misbehaved with Comrades Kishan Lal and Badri Prasad earlier.

The next day we went on strike. The officials were ready for a compromise. It was decided that we were to stay in the barracks at night and would be set free in the daytime, that is, left unshackled in solitary cells. We were happy with this arrangement. Ramnath Suman and more than a dozen political prisoners were already kept in solitary confinement. Suman-ji and his friends had been arrested before us for being naxal sympathisers and now faced charges of criminal conspiracy in a naxalite case.

In the solitary cell we were allowed special privileges of better food and access to books. These cells of the Hardoi jails were actually cleaner and airier than where we came from and hardly looked like solitary cells. We were free and engaged ourselves in discussion on various topics ranging from rural to international politics. Suman-ji was the most well read and the most senior among us. He was a veteran freedom fighter and communist. In his company we came to understand, to an extent, the history of human society and the principles of dialectical materialism. Jokes and entertainment followed serious discussion. Together, we sang the "Internationale", the song written in 1871 by the French worker-poet Eugène Pottier after the defeat of the Paris Commune. Translated into all the major languages of the world, it still inspires the proletariat:

Stand up, damned of the Earth
Stand up, prisoners of starvation
Reason thunders in its volcano
This is the eruption of the end…

Suman-ji was a versatile poet. So we sometimes got together for poetry sessions where each one of us read out poems, and some of us became poets perforce. One such session happened during the Holi of 1971. When his turn came, Kishan-ji tried to get away. He looked tormented and pathetic. Since he was almost unlettered, he could read a newspaper only by a laborious piecing-together of the words. But he was well informed and had a good ear for politics. His appearance did not go well with a poetic sensibility for he looked like a circus dwarf. In fact, he told us that he had even worked for one of the circus companies in South India for a bit. But his exterior was deceptive. He possessed a deep commitment to and faith in the revolution, and his heart overflowed with profound humanity. Kishan-ji begged to be exempted from this torturous exercise of poetry. But we all turned rather unkind and his appeal was ignored. Then suddenly, he sprang up, bent on his knees, and with convoluted funny gestures thoroughly entertained all of us. We rolled with laughter.

By now our trials and hearings had started. Every day hundreds of undertrials were stuffed into police vans and taken to the lower courts. The prisoners were kept handcuffed.

When the van started and left the prison gate, the prisoners chanted the holy names loudly. Upon reaching the court, they were shoved inside small box-like cells and summoned to the respective court when their turn came. These cells were dark, filthy holes covered with cobwebs. Plaster peeled off the walls. It looked as if they had never been cleaned. In a corner, a pair of bricks was placed parallel to each other near an outlet which served as a urinal, and if need be, also for heavier use. The prisoners, all too familiar with the stink, called these cells 'pisspot'.

How many times my friends and I made this pilgrimage I do not recollect. The police guards who waited for us played cards sitting on wooden benches outside the 'pisspot'. The relatives of the prisoners waited outside and watched from a distance. If any prisoner tried to pass on a message to his relatives, the constables glared at him and chased away the relative who would look back longingly before leaving with heavy steps. If police vehicles were not available, the prisoners were made to march from court to prison.

The prisoners were only too happy to walk to court the day they had a hearing. Their relatives would be present at the gate to see them, and got an opportunity to walk along at a slight distance. This way they could speak loudly to convey their messages or tell them about their well-being. More importantly, the prisoners got a chance to breathe the air of freedom beyond the walls of the jail and see something of the world outside. The distance between the court and the jail was less than a kilometer, so a part of the little time they got would be spent in discussing their lawyer or judge or the proceedings. The rest of the time went in chanting together the name of Lord Shiva or some other deity. New prisoners used the opportunity to enquire about court rules and rulings.

According to the orders of the Supreme Court, no undertrial or convict ought to be handcuffed or fettered while being taken from the prison to the courts or otherwise transported between places, for this goes against human dignity. It was not allowed even though it facilitated the policemen's job. I fail to understand who violates these orders—the administration or the Supreme Court itself? But in a country where innocent people are shot dead in false encounters by the police, the dignity of human life is hardly a matter of concern.

During my time in prison, several experiences showed me how the real criminals escape detection. Often, as we returned from court, we noticed the identification parade being held in the prison compound near the main gate. A magistrate, a government prosecutor, the defence lawyer and a jail official would be present. Eleven prisoners were made to stand in a row with the real criminal amongst them. If he had a sign of identification such as a mole, a wart or a scar, this was covered with a strip of paper. Similar strips were plastered on the faces of the other ten persons. At this stage, all these persons were carefully kept out of view of the witness.

Once the parade is ready, each witness is called upon individually to identify the criminal. Escorted by an inmate wearing the yellow prison dress, the witness is frequently hurried along with a kick on the rear. It was no surprise then that a simple villager who came as a witness would be disoriented and terrified before he reached the parade ground.

Once he reached the ground, the judicial magistrate enquired of him details about the person he had come to identify. The magistrate then instructed him to put his hand on the accused as a sign of confirmation. When the witness proceeded to make the identification, a jail official and a yellow-uniformed prisoner walked behind him. Instead of paying attention to identifying the real culprit, the witness was distracted by the fear of being kicked again on the backside by the convict-overseer. In such a situation, often enough the witness either refused to identify the criminal or mistakenly identified the wrong person. If he tried to stop before the real criminal, the overseer and the official walking behind him prodded him to move faster. The witness became nervous and, failing to identify the convict, would move on. Or, to steer clear of all this bother, the criminal might shell out a fat sum as a bribe to be shared by the government prosecutor and the magistrate in collusion with the prison official. I witnessed cases in which the accused was not even present at the parade of the eleven men. Many a time there were instances of misconduct with the female witnesses. In one such identification parade, while the prison official had his back turned to him, a prisoner exposed himself to the female witness.

Our trial lasted seven to eight months. The case was then transferred to the court of the sessions judge. So, till the hearings restarted, our court visits stopped. Many relatives visited me during this period. My father kept his firm determination and assured me that I need not worry, that he would take care of everything. I came to know from my father that my mother had fainted when she got the news of my arrest and had remained distressed for many days.

During this period, a distant relative of mine whom I called mausi (aunt) visited me quite often. Once, when she informed me that a hooligan from her village had tried to misbehave with her pretty daughter, I fumed with anger. I don't have words now to describe that feeling. Who was this aunt? What was my relation to her daughter? It is crucial to tell this story because Munni had a powerful impact on my life later and her memories became my constant companion.

4

Song of love: an interlude

This was at the time I was a student at a college in Kanpur and visited my qasbah, Bangarmau, during the summer vacation. A few of my friends and I were sitting at one of the shops at the crossroads one day when a relative from a nearby village approached me. He wanted me to accompany him to Mallawan police station to lodge an FIR. When I enquired about the details, he pointed towards a woman standing a little distance away and said, "She is my wife's cousin and lives in Manjhiya village. If this job gets done, it would be an act of kindness as there is no one to help her out."

Clad in white, the woman was in her thirties and looked decent. The open, natural life of the village had imparted a glow to her face but her clothes confirmed her widowhood. Goons in her village were trying to take away the seasonal thatching grass grown in her fields. "If this is not stopped, we shall be left with nothing to thatch our roof with. I have four children to look after." As she said this her eyes brimmed with tears. I went to the police station and lodged a report on her behalf with the help of a comrade friend. Later, I came to know that justice had been done and the woman had got back her dues. The hoodlums had been strictly reprimanded and put on notice. All this took place, surprisingly, without the customary 'offerings' made to the police. This made the woman—whom I had started calling mausi—happy and grateful.

After a year or so, one day on my way to another village with a friend, I happened to cross Manjhiya village and decided to rest for a while at mausi's place. Her home was close by and neatly plastered with mud. Happy and surprised to see us, she took us inside. "I waited for you so long. Where have you been all this while? There was a faint touch of reproach in her voice and a little smile played on her face. Noticing her affection for me, I wondered if I had any karmic connection with her in my past lives. Mausi's younger daughter and son watched us with great interest and curiosity. I made them sit beside me on the cot and my friend and I played with them. After offering us water, she left the room. We splashed our hot faces with water and felt refreshed. Our youthful faces looked sunburnt with heat and exertion.

After a little while when mausi returned, her elder daughter followed close behind. A sweet young girl in her early teens, Munni watched us from the corner of her eye, lowered her head and then shyly went into the next room. We did not pay much attention to her. Mausi offered us sherbet to drink and asked her daughter to get the meal ready.

Our plan was to proceed to Bhulbhulia Kheda village near Manjhiya and return the same way. From there, my friend had to leave for elsewhere. Alone by evening, I returned at mausi's request to her house. While Munni was serving the food, a couple of times her eyes met mine. They had the look of innocent surrender. Her siblings had their meal with me. Everything was relaxed and informal. Despite my wish to leave the next day, mausi would not let me go. I couldn't say why but I found myself tied to their modest mud dwelling. Mausi had given me the details of each and every bit of her land and crops. She insisted: "You'll have to visit us frequently as I can no longer look after the farming." She now trusted me wholeheartedly. I too liked her affectionate behaviour.

Just a little way from the door, amid a cluster of trees was a well. The next day, as I was drawing water for my bath, Munni came up from behind me and held the rope. Surprised, when I looked at her, her lips quivered a little and she lowered her eyes. I said, "Leave it. I'll do it." She said, "No, mother will be angry." An introvert by nature, I couldn't argue further. With her supple strong arms, she drew water from the well. For the first time, my eyes lingered with desire on her lovely face. Putting the bucket of water down, she heaved a long sigh of relief and happiness. Sweat sparkled like dewdrops on her round and flushed face displaying the beauty that comes with hard work. A few locks of unruly hair strained to touch her lovely cheeks. When my eyes met hers, I saw rainbow-coloured dreams in them. She lowered her eyes.

By evening the drinking water in the house had been

exhausted. Munni got ready to fetch more water, taking a rope and bucket. I offered to go instead. It did not look proper for her to go out in the dark. Mausi let me go with her. After drawing a bucketful of water, I was about to lift it when Munni took the bucket from me and carried it herself. At my insistence, she let me hold a ring of the bucket while she held the other. "See, don't let go halfway or the water will spill," I said this in a light tone to break the ice but got no response. On the way back we put the bucket down. It was very dark. Trying to control my pounding heart, I looked the other way into the darkness. When I looked back, there was no sign of Munni. I saw her peeping from behind the wall of a dilapidated hut a little away from the path. Seeing me worried, she laughed. Her white teeth sparkled like a glint of lightning in the darkness. I was spellbound, and seemed to sink deeper and deeper into the fathomless ocean of love and longing. Feeling my touch on her shoulder, she slowly rested her head on my chest and said: "Please don't go tomorrow."

"But I have to. I'll come back soon."

"I know you won't," she lovingly asserted her right over me.

"Don't worry, I'll come back soon," I assured her once again.

By the time we reached home with the water, mausi was fast asleep in the courtyard. The children were also sleeping on cots next to hers. Munni shut the door and called out to her mother. But mausi sounded pretty irritable in her sleep and turned over. She was far gone with tiredness. Munni confided that her mother had taken a pinch of opium in the evening, knowing that she could have a good night's sleep since I was there. Munni spread a cot in the room and placed a lota of water close by. I made her sit beside me and we talked through the night. Hesitantly, she confided that her mother was saying I should now find a job. I stroked her hair and sank deep into thought for a while. The next day when I took my leave, mausi made me promise that I would visit them at least once every fortnight. Standing at the threshold of her home, with forlorn eyes Munni watched me go.

Now I had become a frequent visitor to their place. I stayed there for a day or two, and then returned to my work. Mausi sought my advice in all her decisions. And Munni was like a wild deer springing joyously in the forest certain of her happiness and well-being.

How many afternoons we spent on the lonely bank of the river Sai that touched the outskirts of the village. Munni would slip far away in the water like a fish when my hands touched her and would laugh with joy. Wandering amidst the green fields we marvelled at their beauty. Every time Munni emerged laughing from the emerald and yellow mustard field, the tiny yellow flowers clinging to her hair made her look like a pretty forest nymph.

On Ramnavami, mausi made proper arrangements for our visit to Ayodhya. Munni had never seen a town or travelled by train. She was a little surprised but not at all awestruck by the grandeur of modern life. In fact, she could easily adapt to any new situation. Three days later, when we returned via Lucknow, dusk was falling. When we reached the Sai, we realised our mistake—the bottle that mausi had given us to be filled with the holy water of the river Saryu at Ayodhya was empty. Immediately, Munni found a way out—she filled the bottle with water from the Sai.

By now, my family had got wind of my affair. Many of my party comrades criticised me behind my back. But I did not bother. I had great respect and love for them but did not subscribe to their view that as a revolutionary one should avoid women because their presence came in the way of revolution. I believed that if adopting a dull and rigid attitude towards life made one a communist revolutionary, then perhaps I could never become one. Commitment towards a cause can happen only when the heart and the mind are set free. In the dark and difficult times ahead, it was love that made me realise the beauty and simplicity of life, and filled me with total commitment to the cause without distracting me. Bhagat Singh had once said: "As far as love is concerned, I can say that this is only an impulse and nothing else, but this is definitely not beastliness. It never degrades human beings, but this is possible only when love is actually true love."

On hearing about my arrest, mausi cried her heart out and went without food for days together. She came to visit me quite often but never brought along Munni any longer.

5

The verdict in the face of prasad and belief

14 April 1972 was the day of the judgement. We got up early, and as always we chanted the same prayer song, "Utho sone walon sabera hua hai", which the freedom fighters sang on their early morning rounds during the British Raj.

Rise, you who sleep, it is dawn now
Your country beckons you.

Rise, the night of darkness departs
The sun colours the sky molten gold
Come, let us banish the darkness of ignorance
Rise, for it is no time to sleep.

Why laze in the darkness of ignorance?
Rise, you who sleep, it is dawn now.

O Youth of the Nation!
Rise, awake, thou sons of the nation
You, the hope of the future, awake
You, the sons of martyrs, awake.

> See, the darkness of stupor has departed
> Rise, you who sleep, it is dawn now.

After a quick bath we dressed in fresh and crisp clothes we had readied for the occasion. I watched Satyapal apply drops of sticky milk of the gular (cluster fig) leaf to the tips of his moustache and twirl them. Others followed suit. The fine line of moustache on my adolescent face did not let me do so. However, on Satyapal's insistence, I tried to curl up the few hairs of my almost nonexistent moustache. As Kishan Lal, Baijnath and Vibhuti Prasad were clean-shaven, we teased them and enjoyed ourselves at their expense. Chote Lal, being the youngest of the lot, had no moustache.

After the trial at the lower court, we could no longer be taken there with ordinary prisoners. A special police van, with armed constabulary carrying Sten guns in place of the usual muskets, took us there. We were kept waiting in the van near the 'pisspot'. Family members came near the van to meet us. My father had brought the prasad of Hanuman-ji which he offered us. He then applied a vermillion tilak on my forehead which drew a lot of flak from Satyapal. He argued that a communist revolutionary should not allow his father to apply a tilak on his forehead. I was pained by his reaction. At that emotional moment, belief or disbelief in gods and deities or rituals hardly mattered. What was more important for me was to honour the wishes of my father and accept with gratitude my father's love for his son, whatever its mode of expression.

After four in the evening, we were presented before Sessions Judge P.N. Harkouli. Thousands had gathered outside the court. The Provincial Armed Constabulary, called in to cordon off the building, was trying hard to control the unruly mob. Among this huge mass of people were many known and familiar faces. Apart from the relatives, many sympathisers and supporters among the peasants too had arrived in groups. Our comrade Amar Singh's father, Sarju Prasad Pradhan, was a veteran and powerful communist leader. Hundreds of staffs and rifles flashed under the leadership of the sixty-five-year-old, infirm Pradhan-ji. Then my eyes fell on mausi who stood at a distance.

Under the shadow of guns, we were led to the court room. It was jam-packed. Many journalists and senior advocates had especially arrived to hear the verdict on the famous 'Naxal Bakhaura Case'. Because of the likelihood of massive police retaliation, no senior advocate from Hardoi district was ready to fight our case. Lawyers from Unnao and Lucknow districts came as our defence. Surprisingly, it was a young local advocate, Manoharlal, who showed great courage and assisted them.

We were brought near the witness box. In the court room, we stood so close to our family members that we could have easily touched or even whispered to them. My father once again distributed prasad and discreetly blew a little holy ash towards the judge. I then noticed my father take out a strange old piece of clothing tucked into his waist. I realised that it was a tiny silk shirt my mother had preserved carefully. Shackled by superstitions, villagers believe that if some clothing worn by the firstborn on his chhathi (the sixth day after birth) is waved before the judge his mind becomes indecisive and confused. To my knowledge, many of my neighbours and acquaintances had asked my parents for that little piece of my clothing whenever they had to appear before court.

Finally, Judge Harkouli pronounced judgement, finding us guilty of murder. The landlord whose murder we were accused of belonged to Satyapal's village. Therefore, assuming his obvious enmity with him and taking him to be the ring leader, Satyapal was awarded the death sentence and Chotelal, Baijnath, Amar Singh, Shivnath Trivedi, Vibhuti Prasad, Kishan Lal, Mulla, Badri Prasad and I were awarded life imprisonment. The court room echoed with our passionate cries of Inquilab Zindabad, Workers of the World Unite, Hungry Masses Will Not Keep Quiet, Long Live the Armed Revolution!

After the verdict, mausi left without meeting me. I was shocked. This woman, who had willingly offered me all her support and cooperation during the case, never met me again—till I ran into her years later searching for my lost love.

6

A bomb in Hardoi, and the Great Debate

After the judgement, we were taken away amid tight security as before. Dusk was falling. Now we were convict-prisoners. Heavy iron fetters were clamped on our ankles. Our personal clothing was taken away, and ill-fitting, shapeless and filthy uniforms of coarse cloth infested with lice were issued to us. Prison caps were also provided. Satyapal was confined to a solitary cell while the rest of us were sent to the barracks. That night sleep eluded us.

The next morning, we discovered a change in the attitude of the jail authorities. By then, the jailor and the superintendent had taken many rounds and surprisingly enquired after our well-being. I could sense something strange in the air. A warder lowered his voice and said: “Your supporters have blasted a bomb at the bungalow of the judge.”

“What?” I blurted out in shock.

The warder was taken aback by my response and quietly left me. We were disturbed and also curious to learn more about the incident but it was not possible because of the security alert. That day, the CID kept a tight vigil over the family members who visited us in the afternoon. The eatables brought for us were thoroughly inspected. The jailor tapped all the apples with his ruler on suspicion of their being bombs. The next day, the bomb blast at the district judge's bungalow made headlines.

We came to know only later that our party had decided to wage a guerrilla war against all the counter-revolutionary forces of the state—taking the police, the army, and the courts as its representatives. Under this plan, a party worker kept an eye on the bungalow of Judge Harkouli through the night. But he couldn't find an opportune moment to plant the bomb due to the presence of a large contingent of police around the bungalow. Early in the morning, when the policemen dispersed for ablutions, the party worker got near the bungalow, carrying the bomb in a cloth bag. Perhaps he was too terrified to activate it, so he hurriedly dropped the bag near the gate and fled. When an unidentified person going that way saw the bag, he picked it up and the bomb exploded. The injured man was arrested but later released when found innocent. After this incident, the entire Hardoi district was turned into a police camp but the police could not trace our party worker.

Within a week we were shifted to different jails in the state. Chote Lal, Kishan Lal, Mulla and Baijnath were sent to Bareilly Central, and Vibhuti Prasad, Amar Singh, Shivnath Trivedi and Badri Prasad to Fatehgarh jail. Since the police had lodged another case in Lucknow against Satyapal, as explosives had been found in his possession, he was transferred to the Lucknow jail to facilitate the court proceedings. My friends and I were charged with conspiracy to overthrow the government through armed revolt. As a result, I was sent to Unnao jail to stand trial in the Safipur Conspiracy Case.

When the train left Hardoi for Unnao and arrived at my qasbah, Bangarmau, it was dawn. There was a lot of activity on the platform. I was in the custody of armed policemen and sat in fetters near the window. Dozens of acquaintances stopped by to have a look at me. Panic and fear showed on their faces. My younger brother Ganga Singh was also leaving for Kanpur by the same train. When he came to know that I was here, he ran to me and started crying. The policemen allowed him to sit beside me. For the first time I realised that some tenderness remained in the hardest of policemen. They were very sympathetic to my younger brother. After all, ordinary police constables came from the same exploited and oppressed class of our country for whose rights we were fighting. The issue of the killing of policemen during the class enemy annihilation campaign in West Bengal and Bihar came to my mind. Following the Naxalbari Revolt, in order to acquire weapons to bring about a revolution, armed police constables had been killed as part of the 'annihilate the enemy' campaign and their arms taken away. Because of this fear, even the armed traffic police in Calcutta would secure their government-issue weapons with chains.

On reaching the Unnao station, I was taken to jail on foot though it was quite a distance away. I knew for sure that the policemen would pocket the full fare of my transportation from the station to the jail, but I did not say anything. Many of my friends met me on the way and accompanied me for a while. They also offered me good food and sweets at a wayside eatery. Savouring a sweet, scented paan after the meal, I felt like the badshah of Lucknow! I was also happy because among the people who came to meet me were a number of well-known political functionaries and social activists, including leading journalists belonging to the old revolutionary traditions and established families, such as Swatantra Kumar. I remember the look of affection in their eyes. After a while the friends who had accompanied me departed as we walked towards the jail.

At the sight of the Unnao police headquarters that came on the way, I had such a sudden access of rage and shouted slogans of protest. The guards escorting me got alarmed. A number of police constables and officers stationed at the headquarters also came out. Soon, a young deputy superintendent of police appeared with a cap and a black ruler in his hands. In fact, almost every day the police headquarters encountered such incidents and passionate cries of 'Naxalite Zindabad' in different areas of Unnao district. To suppress the naxalite upsurge, the entire district was put under strict police surveillance. It was from Unnao that the naxalite wave had reached Hardoi. The police felt so insecure travelling through the naxalite areas in tongas that they held their rifles at the ready. In the entire district and especially in the rural areas of Safipur, Bangarmau, and Hasanganj, a cat-and-mouse game went on between the police administration and our chief comrades. Under these circumstances, it was natural for the wary policemen to come out on hearing the shout of 'Naxalvaad Zindabad'.

"Who is he? From where have you brought him?" playing with his ruler, the superintendent enquired of the guards.

"Huzoor, the accused's name is Ramchandra Singh. He's from Hardoi jail," replied the guards in panic.

"So it's you who was crying himself hoarse?" The officer spoke in a derogatory tone.

"Shut up, you bastard! Don't you know how to speak?" I yelled at him in English. My face was flushed with anger as I felt insulted. My lips and nose quivered in fury. For a moment, he was stunned. Then, signalling to the guards with his ruler to take me away, he put his cap on, and walked into the headquarters. All along, the guards kept cursing me. One of them said that now the kaptaan of Unnao will write to his counterpart in Hardoi and seek his explanation. Others expressed apprehensions over this incident.

On arriving at the gate of the jail, I again shouted slogans. Later, I was called to the office of the jail superintendent. Removing his spectacles, the superintendent sat at the edge of the chair and stared at me from head to toe.

"Who gave you paan?"he growled.

"I don't think you have called me here to enquire about this."

"Why were you yelling your head off outside the gate?"

"I wasn't doing that. I was registering my protest."

The superintendent thought for a while and then rang the bell. When the warder arrived, he ordered: "Take him to Barrack Number 8."

Barrack Number 8 of Unnao District jail had for the past many years become infamous as the barrack where naxal prisoners were detained. Before my arrival, there were already thirty to forty naxal inmates locked up in that barrack. Among them were my close associates Fakire Lal, Gauri Shankar, Babulal Verma, Lakhpat Rai, Tirthraj Tiwari, Chaudhuri Zahoor Ahmad and Ramswaroop.

I found my colleagues variously occupied in the large, neat and clean barrack—a few were resting, others reading, playing chess or simply talking to each other. At first, no one recognised me. It was only when I smiled that Babulal came over to embrace me. Then all my comrades rushed towards me with great joy and surprise. It was an overwhelming moment, meeting with these comrades who had collectively decided to sacrifice their lives for the socialist struggle. How can I ever forget the glow of happiness and love I saw in their eyes that day! The prison dress of tunic, pajama and cap had completely changed my appearance. They thought that I was one of the convict-sweepers who came to clean the barracks every day. I said, "Yes, of course. All of us brought here are indeed cleaners having been assigned the task of clearing society of class-enemies."

My time in this jail of my home district was peaceful. As a life prisoner, my ankles were to remain in irons for twenty-eight months. Despite being undertrials, my comrades too were kept in fetters which would be removed only after a lot of protest. But Unnao jail was neither as dirty as Hardoi's nor afflicted with rampant corruption and terror.

Here all of us enjoyed each other's company, read, and engaged ourselves in discussions. At times we had ideological differences too. We now realised that even our senior comrades were rather unclear about the ideological direction of our movement.

On my arrival, a long meeting was held which continued till late in the night. I was asked to present a full report and appraisal of the Bakhaura episode. In my ideological assessment, I expressly disagreed with the annihilation of class enemy campaign. Before being sent to jail, I had formed some tactical understanding of revolutionary politics, but one marked by the revolutionary romanticism of a youth. Put into practice, the two aspects began to balance each other out.

During this period, following from the ideologies of Marxism, Leninism and Maoism, my perception was increasingly clear that revolution in India would become possible only once the oppressed classes and communities joined together with the extensive and combined front of workers and peasants. This is the focal point of an agricultural revolution. A discussion along similar lines was going on outside the jails among the senior-most leaders of the party but information of this had not reached the Unnao–Hardoi jails in detail. I held to my belief that individual annihilation would not lead to revolution though it may result in bravery and heroism. To succeed, a revolution requires mass ideological propaganda as it depends on collective effort by the masses and not the random struggle of a handful of activists.

There was complete silence for a moment at the meeting. Breaking the silence, a veteran colleague accused me of turning into a coward and traitor in fear of punishment. This distressed me a great deal. It was not difficult to counter the allegations but at that moment I found it hard to react to the charges of a senior colleague.

I listened to him quietly, but Ramswaroop opposed him and stood up for me. The meeting got articulate and divided itself into two groups—one in favour of continuing the campaign of individual annihilation, and the other opting for the creation of a mass ideological base. The ideological difference that had surfaced among us that night soon turned out to be of a more serious nature.

A few days later, when the challan of Shiv Kumar Mishra-ji, a member of our party's national politburo arrested in the Safipur Conspiracy Case, also reached Unnao, we were overjoyed. The news of his arrival spread like wildfire. The town was abuzz with it. Being a high-profile prisoner, Mishra-ji was kept in a separate cell at the hospital complex. Meanwhile, the famous peasant leader of the Terai region, Vishwanath Tiwari, was also arrested and brought here.

Satyapal's challan, too, had arrived here from Lucknow. Thus, during 1973–74, Unnao jail became the hub of the key naxalite activists.

Our ideological differences were becoming more pronounced. I could see that Mishra-ji wanted to unite us despite them, while knowing quite well that such a compromise was almost impossible to achieve. Ideologically, his sympathies were with our camp. Yet he believed that we were all incomplete in ourselves. He laid special emphasis on acquiring knowledge that would help us adopt the most appropriate radical policy for the masses. He regularly took classes to improve our political understanding and wanted us to be trained to take similar classes for others in future. Under his supervision and guidance, we brought out a handwritten fortnightly newsletter called *Jankranti*. I was made the chief editor of this remarkable entity and brought out many issues. A number of thought-provoking articles and some not-so-good ones got published.

But the fanatical group supporting the enemy annihilation camp started boycotting Mishra-ji's classes. One of the comrades even threatened to shoot Mishra-ji once he was out of jail. Despite appearances to the contrary, there was never personal animosity between the two ideological camps. Vishwanath Tiwari's exterior was hard like a coconut shell, but equally soft and cool on the inside. His nephew (sister's son) Tirathraj was also with us and it was Tiwari-ji who had raised him from a child. Whenever an argument broke out between them, the scene turned interesting. Tiwari-ji invariably lost his temper. With his bloodshot eyes he rolled up his sleeves and, snorting angrily, pounced upon him. Poor Tirathraj could only incoherently put forward his argument, weeping copiously all the while. This frequent scene between Tirath and Tiwari-ji became a regular part of our entertainment. Once they cooled down, I would re-enact the whole exchange for them and all of us rolled with laughter.

During the initial days of the 'annihilate the enemy' campaign, our popularity as Robin Hood-figures reached far and wide in the regions where we operated. However, our reputation also drew many petty dacoits and thieves, who found joining us useful as they had personal scores to settle with others. It was difficult to reform them into sharing our political mindset. Their greed would surface at the slightest pretext. The prospect of abnormalities and deviance creeping into the movement could not be ruled out in a situation where the entire group of leaders was in jail, or because of their absence for any other reason. In these changed circumstances, a number of dacoities took place in the name of naxalism in our area, whereas earlier, through our influence, the activities of such professional dacoits had come to almost a standstill. The situation got so bad at times that a rifle seized from the class enemy would become a bone of contention, with rival claims of ownership from infiltrators who were criminal elements. This led to internecine violence, murder through deceit, and a downright travesty of revolutionary principles.

Let's say a comrade with a criminal background joins the Party. Now, the local landowner or taluqdar's son may well have shared deep fraternal ties with our new-minted comrade, as partners of long standing in various enterprises such as the illegal sale of alcohol. In the course of business-related differences, it may occur that the landlord's son gets violent with the comrade. Seeking revenge, who does the comrade turn to but his naxal contacts, perhaps the very ones who inducted him into the Party. A little later, the said comrade with the help of the Party kills the landlord's son and, for good measure, an elderly member of the landlord's family as well. He now emerges a hero of the 'annihilate the enemy' campaign and a naxal leader in his own right. This is no hypothetical storyline but a general illustration of the impasse in which the Party found itself, facing the swift dissolution of revolutionary politics on the ground.

By no means was ideological and operational confusion restricted to the grass-roots level. It went all the way up to international communist politics of the time and the bitter discord that existed between the governments of the USSR and China. The divergence between them came to the fore after Nikita Krushchev's denunciation of Stalin at the Twentieth Congress of the Communist Party of the USSR, on 25 February 1956. At the Congress, Krushchev also proposed a policy of peaceful co-existence with the imperialist West. In a nutshell, the official Soviet position was increasingly non-interventionist and placed its trust in the idea that the pace of history could not be forced, that revolution would come about ineluctably—as the capitalist system buckled under the weight of its contradictions—and the transition to a socialist order need not be violent. Krushchev's volte-face caused consternation across the communist world. In 1963, the Communist Party of China, under the leadership of Mao Tse-tung, released nine documents denouncing the Krushchev line as a betrayal of communist solidarity and as revisionism, or the weakening of revolutionary ardour.

This division—termed the Great Debate—was to split communists in India as well. In the wake of the Twentieth Congress, the Communist Party of India (CPI) had followed the Soviet lead. However, discontent with this position brewed among both leaders and cadre. In a kneejerk attempt to suppress dissent, thirty-two top leaders of the National Board were expelled from the Party. These leaders—including Jyoti Basu, Harkishen Singh Surjeet and E.M.S. Namboodiripad—formed a new party, the CPI (Marxist) in 1964. Even the CPM, as it was known, fell short of the expectations of workers and cadre. Instead of taking a clear stand on the Great Debate, its leadership cleaved to a safe middle path and in turn expelled radical leaders at the regional and local levels who refused to submit to the party line. Thus was born the CPI-ML (Marxist-Leninist), in 1969.

The tumult within the communist movement was matched by a time of great economic hardship in India, marked by foodgrain shortages, chronic poverty, hunger and unemployment. This formed the backdrop to the Naxalbari uprising. In the northern region of West Bengal, the owners of tea gardens and jotedars (wealthy peasants) had captured vast tracts of land. The United Front government of the state, which included a component of the CPM, refused to act against the land grab and redistribute land to the peasantry. As part of a strategy of repression, eleven people—among them both rebels and children—were shot dead by the police on 25 May 1967. This atrocity gave the immediate spark to the Naxalbari uprising. Thousands of students and youth converged to organise the peasantry. The influence of the Cultural Revolution, then underway in China, was clearly visible in the organisational and ideological leadership of Comrade Charu Mazumdar. As the Cultural Revolution peaked in China, Chinese radio hailed the naxal revolt as an act of comradeship.

The result of this influence was that, in the second phase of the naxal revolt, its leaders blindly imitated whatever percolated down to them from China, and the conditions of India were analysed on the basis of the Chinese revolution. At the time of its communist revolution in 1949, China was a semi-colonised country, while much of its territory was in the custody of feudal war lords. This characterisation was now applied wholesale to India. At the Seventh Party Congress held in 1970 under the leadership of Charu Mazumdar, India came to be projected as a semi-colonial and semi-feudal system, ripe for revolution. The advocacy of tactics of long-term guerilla warfare and the slogan of 'annihilate the enemy' followed from here. Parliamentary process was no longer considered a viable strategy. The Party had to develop an underground wing and use both legal and illegal tactics according to its needs and the prevailing circumstances.

After the Party Congress, voices rose in protest against extremism, and the Party splintered between the views of the gradualists and those who favoured an ultra-left position, a rift that has not healed since.

7

Munni, my pillar of strength

As an undertrial, my stay at the Hardoi jail had been full of uncertainty and deep turmoil. We, the political prisoners, consciously tried to keep ourselves in a positive frame of mind. But when we reflected on the future, all kinds of troubling thoughts came to us at night, as nightmares and waking dreams. In order not to lapse into such a state we kept ourselves occupied with reading and discussions.

Once I arrived at the Unnao District Jail, the scene changed completely. There was a new freedom. I could receive food from home, walk freely in the barrack compound, and read without any anxiety or fear. The facilities which we legally deserved were provided to us immediately by the jail authorities. As the whole district was aware of our political movement, the jail administration treated us with sensitivity.

Our trials in the Safipur case began with Mishra-ji's arrival. My father was often present at the court. Unnao being close to Kanpur, I was also visited by friends and comrades. My mother and grandmother too came to meet me. We were given enough time for these meetings which took place below the water tank at the gate of our barrack's courtyard. When any of us had visitors, all of us were allowed to be out of the courtyard for a while. At times, our visitors came inside the barracks out of curiosity to have a look.

One afternoon, a supervisor informed me that I had visitors waiting in the courtyard. On coming out of Barrack Number 8, I found my father and touched his feet. Then I spread a blanket for him to sit and asked about his unexpected arrival. He pointed towards the water tank. To my disbelief, I saw Munni standing against the pillar of the tank.

I forgot myself and just stared at her. These two years had imparted a rural robustness to her, but her eyes betrayed pain. Like a typical village girl, she was casually draped in a coarse sari that stopped short of her ankles. Her feet were naked and dusty. But her soft and shapely legs could be seen through the sari. She looked charming, and tired, like a village girl leaning for a while against a mahua tree on a hot summer afternoon after the day's hard labour in the field. At my calling, she came closer and squatted on the ground. Despite trying hard to control herself, she wept.

"When did she come here?" I asked my father.

"Yesterday," he said.

Mausi had waited for me till the judgement on my case. After the verdict, she started looking for another boy as a prospective husband for Munni. Munni was unwilling to go along with this and threatened to hang herself if forced into marriage, so her mother quietened down. She told me that she had left home the previous day, along with some

Muslim women from Manjhiya who were leaving for the Urs festival at Ganj Muradabad. Then, she took a bus and reached Bangarmau, four kilometres away from her home and found my father at the wholesale market for jaggery. My father was surprised to see her and brought her the next day to meet me.

In the presence of my father I could offer her only words of consolation, but she shed tears to see my feet in heavy iron fetters. That day, after the meeting, my father left her in Kanpur with my mother and grandmother and went back to Bangarmau. After a week or so, she came to meet me again, with my mother and grandmother. They asked my other friends about their well-being while I got a chance to speak to Munni. I told her that she shouldn't bind herself to my uncertain future. In a soft but firm voice she said, "Did you leave me that day to say all this?"

The next time she visited, she was dressed in the finery of a new bride resplendent with vermillion in the parting of her hair. This time she had worn her sari properly, her feet were coloured with mahawar and she wore silver toe rings in them. My aunt (mother's sister) had made her wear a few pieces of jewellery. I was surprised to see the flowering of her youth in such a short time. She looked happy and contented. When her eyes met mine, she smiled shyly and slowly lowered her eyes. Dressed in coarse khadi pajama and a red striped half-tunic, my feet shackled in heavy iron fetters, I stood there deep in thought reflecting on my misfortune. At this moment, the memory of the past, the situation at present and the apprehension for the future—all got muddled in my mind.

For days together, the conflict of accepting Munni as my wife in my present state raged inside me. I was responsible for her future for she was now a part of me but at the same time, I was also disturbed. My friends never refrained from making fun of me. To be so anxious about a girl cannot be the sign of a true revolutionary, they said. If being a revolutionary meant being insensitive to inner consciousness, feelings and sympathies, if it is an externally imposed state of mind, then truly I wasn't one. I loved Munni with all my heart and soul and wanted a life for her that was free from my uncertain future. But I could see that there were no signs of anxiety, fear or doubt about the future in her. Her firm determination gradually persuaded me to accept her as my wife.

I now started calling her by her real name, Ramdulari. She usually lived with my mother and grandmother in Kanpur. Every week and sometimes after a gap of a couple of days, she came to meet me accompanied by one of her siblings. She was no longer a rustic girl but a graceful young woman. She had adjusted to town life with ease. During her visits, I tried to refine her taste and motivate her to read. Within a short time, she absorbed a lot and soon read Maxim Gorky's *Mother.* She liked the character of Powell very much.

Almost a year had passed. Mausi remained displeased with her. When Munni lived in Manjhiya with her mother, a case of molestation was lodged against the local zamindar's agent who had tried to misbehave with her. The case was still pending in the Hardoi court. In order to trap Munni, her mother managed to get a bailable summons issued to her as a witness in this case. Munni appeared before the court at Hardoi accompanied by many of my women relatives, fifty to sixty armed friends and my supportive father. This was more than mausi had bargained for. On seeing them, the dozen or so of her supporters and the police sub-inspector disappeared. I was happy to know that when mausi came to meet her, Munni behaved decently without holding any grudge against her.

Soon, all my comrades in and outside the jail accepted Ramdulari as my wife with due respect and honour. They were concerned for her and offered all kinds of support. The new environment greatly influenced her and she became confident. She was now praised in the revolutionary communist belt. Love made me sensitive towards her and she was ready for a political life, even to sacrifice her life. During the visiting hours, we managed to steal a few moments of privacy to express our heartfelt feelings for each other. A couple of times she visited me in my barrack. During those lighter moments my friends called her 'Bhabhi' and made all kinds of false allegations against me to tease her. Her tinkling laughter echoed in the barrack as if challenging the red brick walls—equally those of their dogma and of the state. Her love had become the pillar of strength in my life.

8

A police mutiny and support from outside

In the Bakhaura case, our defence lodged an appeal at the Allahabad High Court against the decision of the Hardoi Sessions Court. When we were summoned for the hearing of this appeal, all the comrades from Unnao, Fatehgarh and Bareilly were shifted to Naini Central Jail, Allahabad. Satyapal, with his death sentence, was put into the 'condemned cell', and we were sent to the small and filthy cells of Malviya Bhavan. We were let out twice or thrice a day for short spells. Meals, including our breakfast of boiled gram, were passed through the barred windows. Every evening we were shifted to different rooms and our bedding and clothes were thoroughly searched. This was our first taste of the Central Jail.

We often spoke to the convict guards posted at our prison cell. Some said they had been there for eighteen years, others for twenty years or twenty-five. One of the prisoners had been shot dead before our arrival in Naini. We were told that he was trying to escape. It was a harrowing place to be in.

I came to know some details soon enough. Two notorious culprits Achhan and Bachchan had a serious disagreement with the jailor over some issue. They threatened to fix the jailor once they got out. A few days later, Bachchan's attempt to escape was foiled with a bullet that killed him. An inquiry followed and the jailor was transferred to the open-air prison in Ghurma, where the prisoners were used as stone quarrying labour. The vindictive jailor was shot and killed here. This was widely regarded as the Achhan–Bachchan gang's revenge for the murder.

One day when the superintendent came on his rounds I told him that as we were political prisoners we couldn't be held in cells. He refused to listen to me and said that he knew only two types of prisoner—one, the undertrials, and the other, the convicts. To him, political prisoner did not mean anything. I had to inform him that when a person is sent to jail because of political reasons, no one misbehaves with him; rather he is provided certain special facilities. Even ordinary prisoners here were deprived of facilities they had every right to receive. But he moved on without comment.

A month later, we were sent back to our respective prisons. The high court converted Satyapal's death sentence to life imprisonment and a co-convict, Mulla, was released. The rest of the punishment was upheld. While returning to Unnao, Satyapal and I were provided only an old and tattered blanket to cover ourselves against the biting cold of late December. The constables accompanying us occupied the cushioned seats of the first-class coach while we were made to sit on the floor. Curling up like street dogs, we huddled closer to each other trying somehow to fend off the terrible cold. All the way from Allahabad to Kanpur, an elderly lady from a well-to-do family shot annoyed glances at us.

In the meantime, the police and the Provincial Armed Constabulary (PAC) of Uttar Pradesh had revolted. Pitched battles were fought between the battalions of armed forces (called in to make the mutineers surrender) and the PAC at Kanpur, Lucknow, Barabanki and Ramnagar. Finding themselves surrounded by the armed forces, many jawans of the PAC fled with their arms. A leader from the police council issued an appeal to the policemen, analysing the political scenario and exhorting them to join hands with the revolutionaries among the masses and uproot the whole power structure. Several bundles of pamphlets reached us, which we distributed among the constables who escorted us to court for our trials, and we raised slogans supporting the police–PAC revolt. Officials at the Local Investigation Unit kept an eye on our activities as they were onto the fact that we were distributing pamphlets. Fearing an untoward incident, the government brought to a halt all hearings of cases related to the naxalites who had been kept at the Unnao jail. Instead of taking us to courts outside the precincts of jail, our cases were to be taken up within the jails. We vehemently protested against this.

Meanwhile, R.K. Garg, a senior advocate at the Supreme Court, was trying to moot the idea of forming a committee at the national level to fight for the release of naxal prisoners.

During those days, to raise one's voice against the atrocities committed on naxal prisoners was an act of courage. Garg's initiative found many supporters among politicians such as Krishna Kant, Chandra Shekhar and George Fernandes, Khwaja Abbas Ahmad and Hansraj Rahbar among the leading litterateurs. Garg came to meet the naxal prisoners in Unnao jail. Discussions on several issues took place between him and Mishra-ji. Mr Garg impressed us with his decency. He even refused to sit on the chair brought for him by the jail authorities and sat cross-legged with us on the cement berth. As he spoke, he played with my iron fetters. He had also brought along packets of cigarettes, boxes of coffee and biscuits, dry and fresh fruit and some magazines in Hindi and English, all of which lasted us many days.

In the meantime, Charan Shandilya and K.C. Tyagi from Delhi, supporters of the naxalite cause, visited us. They had formed the All-India Revolutionary Youth Brigade with Ram Asrey Verma, and also brought out a monthly journal *Yuvanak* from Delhi. *Yuvanak* had become quite popular with the progressive youth of North India. Tyagi took one of my essays to be published in *Yuvanak*, in which I had tried, with guidance from Mishra-ji, to make a reassessment of the roles of Gandhi and the Congress during the period of the nationalist struggle. Part of my argument was that the demolition of public statues of Gandhi and other nationalist figures by leftist protesters in West Bengal was not faithful to the values of the Cultural Revolution, and that political and ideological criticism be kept separate from personal insult. The essay drew quite a response from the radical communists of Uttar Pradesh. The same issue of *Yuvanak* carried the much discussed 'Last Letter' of Charu Mazumdar and its political analysis by Mishra-ji. The analytical essay by Mishra-ji gave new direction to the rethinking that was going on among naxalites throughout the country. We came to know only later that Tyagi had joined Charan Singh's camp, and his involvement in the Suresh–Sushma episode appeared in the newspapers.[1] I felt strange, especially as I remembered his gentle behaviour and commitment.

After the suppression of the police–PAC revolt, once again I was sent to the court. After a long trial, we were freed from the charge of treason. The police now implicated me in false charges of dacoity and other crimes, and initiated new cases against me. Amazingly, the police claimed these crimes were committed by me while in jail. To stand trial on these fraudulent charges, I was again remanded to Hardoi jail. My wife accompanied me on the short bus journey till Bangarmau. The bus stopped there for a while. Learning of my arrival, many people flocked around our bus. I was fortunate to get a glimpse of my father's hometown once again.

---

1 In 1978, pictures of Suresh Ram (son of former defence minister Jagjivam Ram) having sex with Sushma Chaudhury, a Delhi University student, were printed in *Surya*, a magazine published by Maneka Gandhi. Tyagi, general secretary of Yuva Janata in 1978, and considered to be close to Janata Party's Choudhary Charan Singh, was instrumental in the distribution of the photographs.

At Hardoi, I was back in those cells where I had spent almost two years. A prominent leader of the Uttar Pradesh Police Council, Ram Ashish Rai, was detained there. A few days after my arrival, Ram Asrey Verma was also brought there under the Security Act. I was meeting him after a long time. We got along well with each other. After a month and a half, I was sent back to the Unnao jail. All the false charges against me had been revoked.

From Unnao, I was sent to the Fatehgarh Central Jail to serve the term for life imprisonment. I had fond memories of my days at the Unnao jail in the company of my friends and comrades. Mishra-ji, Chaudhuri Zahoor Ahmad and other comrades had been released before my challan. Learning of my departure, all of them came to meet me at the Unnao railway station. Comrades Chandrika Prasad and Shambhu Dayal accompanied me to Kanpur. Shambhu was much younger to me and I had a lot of affection for him. He remained sad all through the way.

The train reached Kanpur around six or seven in the evening. The next train to Fatehgarh was two or three hours later. Shambhu had informed my parents of the journey. At the Kanpur station, my mother, grandmother, maternal uncles and aunts, brother, wife and others waited for me. They all wept for me and I tried to console them. Looking at my heartbroken mother, I struggled to keep my emotions in check. My mother had brought parathas which she fed me with her hands. At that moment, I felt that if my mother could sit with me like this, I would readily pass my remaining years in fetters. I left my mother and all the others with great sorrow. But my wife was adamant about accompanying me to the jail. Finally, my mother and grandmother agreed to let her join my brother and me to Fatehgarh.

The train was speeding through the early dawn. The armed constables sitting around me had dozed off. My younger brother, Kailash, too was trying to catch some sleep on the upper berth. Finding a quiet moment, my wife hid her face in my chest and cried. I remembered the days spent with her in Manjhiya when she would hide her fair, flushed face in my bosom and laugh. After reaching Fatehgarh jail the next day, I asked my brother and wife to return so that they could find a connecting train easily. They left with heavy hearts.

9

The paltaiyya torture and Gupta-ji's cavalcade

All the jails of Uttar Pradesh that I was placed in had more or less the same layout. Their internal plan differed only in terms of the available space. In all jails, just after the main gate is the office of the jail superintendent, and next to it that of the chief jailor. Then, after crossing one or two big gates and some open space, comes a dalaan or courtyard—which may be large or small. The courtyard leads to all the circles via galleries. The circles hold the barracks where prisoners live. The structure of the circles and galleries varies with the size of the jails.

Fatehgarh Central Jail is the largest in Uttar Pradesh. Around two thousand prisoners are on its roll. Built in the year 1865, it has more than a hundred and fifty officials and employees. Its dalaan is huge, from where lead all the pathways to the circles. Even the circles have plenty of space and the compounds of the barracks are large. Besides, the jail has factories on its premises. This was a change from the smaller jails I had thus far known. Factories are a feature of the larger or central jails where long-term prisoners predominate, whereas only undertrials who come and go (on bail) are found in the smaller jails like Hardoi.

A number of small industries function inside the jail where prisoners are forced to work. The compounds of the factories are spacious. There are green shady trees in and around the circle and the factories. The atmosphere is nonetheless one of fear and oppression, and the prisoners slog like beasts of burden. Tent manufacturing is one of the major industries here. Rugs, carpets, cloth and so on are also produced. In addition, the jail has a huge agricultural farm.

This jail is a pilgrimage site on account of the many brave warriors of the independence struggle who were incarcerated here, among them well-known revolutionaries such as Bishambar Dayal Tripathi, Shiv Kumar Mishra and Balgangadhar Tripathi. The rebel, Manindra Nath Bannerjee sacrificed his life while on hunger strike here. In independent India, the walls of this jail remained witness to many prisoners who were innocent or who had taken the law into their hands upon being refused justice.

The moment I reached the gigantic gates of the jail, the cry 'Inquilab Zindabad' escaped my lips. The guards at the gate were startled. A voice hollered from the inside: "Quiet!" With this shout, a small door at the gate rattled open and the head warder of the jail, Pandit Chotelal, moved menacingly towards me twirling his moustaches and waving a long, thick cane in his hand. A man in his mid-fifties, he had a thickset body of average build, a salt-and-pepper handlebar moustache—the hair on his scalp dyed black—and the agile bearing of a youth. In short, his appearance was that of a seasoned goon.

"I'm still outside the jail and I have every right to shout a slogan," I said.

"I must remind you that you are now within the jail precincts." His eyes burned and he shook with anger at my audacity. Seeing this, I became certain that I was in for a special welcome. As soon as I entered he handed me over to two inmates and left, seething. He was sure that these two, notorious for their brutality, would set the foolish newcomer to rights in no time at all.

"Why were you shouting?" The two hulking men with dull but cruel eyes rolled up their sleeves and stomped towards me like testy bulls.

"It was for my party and for the masses of my country."

"What masses? Which party?" One of them asked.

"The workers' party! The Communist Party (Marxist–Leninist), the naxal party."

"So, you are a naxal. Which is your home district?"

Hearing the name Unnao, he became hesitant. (Later I came to know that he too belonged to Unnao.)

"Go and sit there quietly. If you shout slogans in the jail anymore, you'll be thrashed. This place is ruled by Gupta-ji. You hear? Gupta-ji!"

I took my bag and sat in a corner. Then I was searched. I was asked to remove my clothes and my slippers. These were thoroughly scrutinised. The two journals in my cloth bag—*Point of View* and *Mainstream*—were seized. After the search, I was handed over to an inmate and sent to the circle.

The inmate told me that I had been let off quite easily. Newly arrived tough criminals are made to remove all their clothes and even their rectum is checked to see if they have hidden a roll of currency notes there. I was shocked out of my senses. I couldn't credit this story but other inmates removed my doubts.

The inmate-supervisor informed me that a while back some farmers from the rural area of Kanpur (East) had been jailed for their alleged involvement in the agitation over the supply of irrigation water. They too had shouted slogans at the gate. But once inside the prison, they were roughed up by the hardened inmates. A boy among them suffered an injury to his ears and blood had gushed out from his mouth.

I too recalled an incident told by a freedom fighter. During the British period the prisons did not allow even tobacco or beedis within the jail premises. But these were smuggled in with the help of cleaners or the cart-men who removed garbage in their bullock carts. The scavengers hid the contraband in containers of human excreta, while the cart-men concealed it in the rectum of their bullocks. Once, a bullock happened to excrete in the precincts of the Naini jail and out came the beedis and tobacco rolled inside waxed covers. When this came to light, the cart-man was penalised and the prisoner for whom it was meant was brutally beaten up. I wondered if there was any difference between the jails of the British period and those of today.

Soon I met comrades who had arrived before me: Amar

Singh, Badri Prasad, Vibhuti Prasad and one Mangatraj-ji who was involved in another naxal case. We were all prisoners to be kept under strict vigilance. Here, we had to slog harder: from unloading coal off the truck to taking care of the jailor's garden. Then I was sent to the First Circle to work on the Amber Charkha. I was given a blanket, a mat, a plate and bowl (tasla-katori). The inmate-storekeeper warned me that if any of these items were lost, I would undergo the paltaiyya, a torturous punishment in which, at the instruction of the official, the prisoner was thrown to the ground and the soles of his feet caned by five or six inmate-warders or senior inmates. After every thirty to forty strikes, the battered and bruised inmate was made to run to restore the blood circulation in his leg. After a few rounds, he was again thrown on his back and made to undergo the same torture. This cycle would continue for some time. Called the paltaiyya or talua parade in prison jargon, it was considered at the time to be the easiest punishment at Fatehgarh jail. The prisoner would recover after applying warm mustard oil on his swollen soles, though his spirit might be shattered for life.

The inmates mostly kept their tasla-katori with themselves. Every morning after the barrack opened and the head count was done, they finished their ablutions and then assembled in the ground of their respective circle, to be counted again in pairs before the deputy jailor. It was mandatory to have the tasla-katori in hand for the jailor's inspection.

In the meantime, the warders locked the barracks. After

the counting of prisoners in the circle—or chakkar ginti, as it was known—followed by breakfast and prayers, they were sent to their respective kamaan or section. Groups of prisoners doing the same work were known as the kamaan for that job. Prisoners employed in making strings from coconut or jute fibre (baan) were known as baan kamaan, those spinning thread on a charkha or spindles the charkha kamaan, and so on.

When the inmates left the barracks they took with them the necessary items for the day. If someone had extra goods such as jaggery, gram, bundles of beedi, ghee or oil, he would put them into a cloth bag and hang it from resourcefully procured nails, above his berth in the barrack. The biggest problem for the prisoners was to hide articles which were forbidden under the rules of the jail authority but essential to daily life: say, matchsticks or a lighter for beedis, a small knife to slice the onions or fruit brought by visitors, a blade to shave or clip nails with, a small mirror or just a broken piece of one to see their face in, etc. A matchbox or lighter was tied discreetly to one end of the prisoner's gamchha (shoulder cloth) and the gamchha slung casually over the shoulder. The lighter could not be left behind in the barrack as the prisoners frequently needed a clandestine smoke. Sometimes, they would secrete away a few matchsticks and a bit of the strike-surface on their person. No prisoner kept a knife with a handle. Instead a thin strip of iron did the duty, sharpened on a stone or brick and hidden in the gaps of their individual berths. Similarly, they wrapped the shaving blade and a piece of mirror in a cloth and hid it. Not all prisoners had these objects. Those who didn't, borrowed from the others. As the barracks were locked in the morning and unlocked at a scheduled time after the prisoners returned from work, the fear of losing these possessions did not arise.

It was a real possibility that the tasla-katori might be stolen by the warders themselves or sold off to a jail employee for a couple of packs of beedis or a packet of tobacco. I remembered the deputy jailor of Hardoi who instructed his goons to steal the utensils of the prisoners and then threatened them with the paltaiyya. To save his skin, the victim had to send home for money as an offering to the sahib. At the smallest pretext, this sahib would extract a penalty of five rupees from the prisoners.

I observed the same practice among officials and employees across all the jails. In the Fatehgarh Central Jail, it was an everyday occurrence for a prisoner to be brutally beaten up at the slightest pretext. Nor was it unusual to find an inmate with broken bones or throwing up blood. The inmates' lore of the sahib's terror inflated it still more. They held that even leaves were stilled, plants withered at his touch and crows forgot to caw when he was on his rounds.

The entire circle was cleaned up on the day of the monthly parade. Drains were sprinkled with lime and the circle with red brick powder. Fatehgarh's band was known to be the best among the jails of Uttar Pradesh and had secured second position in the inter-state competition. The jail band did not play every day. It came into action before the grand entrance of the Bada Sahib G.L. Gupta at the weekly parade, or to welcome top officials and persons of distinction on a visit. The members of the band team were delegated to one kamaan or another and included in the band when the need arose. Occasionally, they relinquished their work to practice. The band was led by the inmate Kalyan Singh.

When it played, the inmates forgot all their woes for a while, in the soulful music. The moment it stopped, all of us sat up straight at our assigned places, arms stretched over knees, palms facing out. It was time for the sahib's visit. I could see the terror of death in the eyes of the prisoners. Then a voice would boom out: Khabardaar! Beware!

On hearing this, all the inmates stood up with their history-sheets in hand. The head warder Chotelal was in a crisp, clean uniform and, with a click of the heels, snapped to attention near the gate. My heartbeat increased. The bada sahib entered. He was an unprepossessing youngish man in his early forties. Wearing black sunglasses, he walked with arrogance. Behind him came twenty or so inmate-wardens, senior inmates, and warders with batons in their hands. Some prison officials and employees followed. A senior inmate held a beautiful umbrella over him while another fanned him with a chanwar. His stateliness was no less than a king's.

Jails are ruled by the administrative officials but their rules cannot be implemented by them alone. Prisoners, too, are used for this. Those in the bada sahib's retinue enjoyed special privileges and were known by their designations: among them the nambardar, writer, chhuttiwan or labour supervisor, and most important, the pakkas—chosen by the jail superintendent from among the nambardars. A prisoner is eligible to become a nambardar upon completing a quarter of his sentence. Not everyone gets to be a nambardar, though. It also depends on the needs of the jail and the whims of the superintendent. A nambardar can move around within the jail on work. He is placed on duty at important places to keep watch.

In district jails, the number of pakkas is generally one or two whereas in central jails there may be four to five. They are assigned the duty of keeping watch over the jail, that is, over the prisoners and all the places deemed important or sensitive. The pakka who is peon to the jail superintendent or who gets to keep watch over the main gate is considered the most powerful. Two pakkas were posted at the main gate of the Fatehgarh Central Jail, in alternating watches. Another pakka was the peon of the jail superintendent, G.L. Gupta. While the actual peon of the superintendent is a warder, the pakka at the main gate had more influence than any warder.

These pakkas had the undeclared freedom to cook for themselves and to access supplies from the market. They were usually not locked up in the barrack but remained outdoors at night in the call of duty. The pakka of the superintendent is generally called 'sahib ka pakka' and accompanies the superintendent when he is on his rounds. The power of the pakkas at the gate and the sahib ka pakka is recognised not just by the prisoners but also by jail employees, officials and even the superintendent. The sahib ka pakka is his eyes and ears. Although he is not a declared 'trustee'—such as exist in the West—his status is no lesser. He has the power to resolve minor complaints and conflicts of the prisoners on his own. The reason for his status is the large scale corruption endemic to jails. If the jailor wants to smuggle out finished goods from the factories within, such as rolls of cloth, wooden items or rations, he will have to go through the main gate where the pakka has the authority to search or question him. It simply is not possible to run a profiteering racket of any kind without the pakka's knowledge and complicity. As a result, even jail officials like to keep the sahib ka pakka in good humour.

The morning of my first parade I beheld this magnificent panoply of state headed in my direction: the bada sahib himself, his fly whisk and umbrella bearers, the echelon of pakkas and nambardars bearing lathis, and jail officials.

As soon as he was near me, I said, "Sir, I have a request to make." He stopped for a moment. Two inmates at once seized my arms. The sahib let his gaze travel over me.

"Yes, what do you have to say?"

"I arrived here four days ago. I am a naxal prisoner. I am facing some problems. Would you care to listen to me?" I said politely.

"What's your problem? What do you want?"

"Please shift my friends and me elsewhere. We want

to spend our time here in reading and please stop the hard manual labour that we are forced to do."

"But you all are leaders of the masses, aren't you? You should stay with them. Why do you want to be away from them?"

"Because there isn't any arrangement or atmosphere conducive to study. At the moment, I don't think we have enough space for that."

"You may ask your visitor to get you some writing material but you will have to show whatever you write to the jailor regularly. As far as physical labour is concerned, I expect fourteen balls of cotton spun on the Amber Charkha from the workers. But for you I will make it five, which is the rule."

"Thank you."

"You all want to annihilate the capitalists. Do you consider me one?"

"We consider you a bureaucrat who is a pillar of this entire capitalist system. As for our ideology with regard to capitalism and the difference between abolishing capitalism and annihilating capitalists—that's a long story."

"Hmm." And he moved away.

The news that the sahib did not punish me spread like wildfire among the prisoners. No prisoner had ever dared to speak with him. They were also surprised to know that I was asked to spin only five balls of cotton, and that he himself had said this was unbelievable. In fact, anyone who spun less than fourteen balls was in for a hammering. This applied to prisoners engaged in other trades as well. Every day defaulters were punished brutally. From that day, the inmates assumed a deferential attitude towards me. They considered me a powerful don.

That night, after the barracks were closed, I could hardly sleep and remembered my mother, my wife and other family members. My mother's face flashed before my eyes and my heart went out to my wife who had suffered silently all this time. I also felt sad for my young brothers. How silent and glum the tunnel-like barrack looked in the dull light of lanterns. Deep in slumber, the inmates, covered in torn old blankets, looked like corpses. Only when an elderly inmate shook with a bout of phlegmy coughing was I convinced about the presence of life in the barracks. I tossed and turned in my berth and a flood of thoughts kept me awake all through the terrible night.

The next morning, when we returned from our workshops, the circle jailor summoned me to his office. He held a long letter in his hand. He looked sharply at me and said, "Mister, here's a letter from the officials of your district with orders that you should be kept under special security because you are a dangerous naxal." I was surprised. Then he entrusted me to a dark, giant-like inmate with instructions to keep vigilant twenty-four hours. Now I couldn't speak with anyone. Anyone who wished me was headed for trouble. He escorted me to the workshop. At night I was under his tight surveillance. When I went to relieve myself, he planted himself with his baton outside the lavatory door. In brief, he never left my side for a moment. There was a special instruction that I must not be allowed to read or write as the jail authorities feared that I might write something inflammatory and provocative and smuggle it out. They were still more apprehensive that I may leak out information on the rampant corruption and dread that prevailed in the jail. Every day, before the barracks were locked up for the night, all my belongings were thoroughly inspected. Despite this, I secretly scribbled letters in the toilet and sent them out to my comrades.

This senior inmate or pakka, called Upadhyaya, who kept vigil over me, was actually stupid, simple and stubborn. One moment, he would glare at me with anger, yell and curse me, but the next moment he would grin and roar with laughter. He never hurt me or anyone in the prison. Gradually, things became easier for me. Three or four months later, he was removed from my security.

10

'To blast your ego, you sinner!'

I had heard a lot of legends about prison life during my childhood. If you are slow at work, expect a kick on your butt. Inmates are made to sweep and mop, they are served water hyacinth weed in place of green vegetable, the flour for rotis is kneaded by foot, while the rotis are brushed with a broom, and so on. All these horrifying details warned us to be careful lest the same fate befall us. Had we known the reality then, we wouldn't have ever imagined prison in such pallid terms.

The true stories of Fatehgarh jail were far more horrible by any stretch than the hearsay of childhood. The prisoners lived in constant fear of the random visits and unscheduled rounds of the superintendent, G.L. Gupta, accompanied by his train of twenty or so nambardars, hardened criminals or pakkas, and warders. It was as if a feudal lord and his war machine were on the move. He bashed up any inmate that he met on the way. Whoever he pointed at, baton blows rained on him for no rhyme or reason. Surprise assaults were aimed at inmates waiting their turn outside the toilets or hand-pumps or even while being served food. Invariably every day battered and bruised inmates were taken to the hospital, their blood dripping.

Initially, inmates were prevented from conversing with their fellow inmates, turning their face towards them while lying down, or even lighting their beedi by another's. Once, all the stuff of the two thousand odd prisoners that family members had brought for them was seized and burnt. This included oil, jaggery, roasted gram, ghee, beedis, chillies, tobacco and other precious possessions the prisoners had lovingly stored in their filthy cloth-bags and bundles.

Every inmate dreaded being called to the 'gumti' by the bada sahib, which was as terrible as being called to the gallows. Here the convicts were hung upside down from a neem tree and beaten up. To return intact from the gumti was next to impossible. Brutally bashed up, they were dumped into the hospital, given only basic first aid and sent back to their circles to work. Sometimes instructions were issued to award them a fixed number of blows before they were put to work.

A convict named Narayan Singh was awarded ten baton blows every day before being set to work. After reaching the factory, Narayan Singh would lie down on the floor, raise his feet and suffer the blows raining ruthlessly on his soles. Sobbing, he would find the strength to begin his work without a word. This atrocity continued for months together. Even his moustaches were pulled out on one occasion and stored in a box. Who knows, it may still be lying in the jail storeroom.

These atrocities were inflicted upon those who refused to barter their pride for anything. Secretly warming oneself by the logwood fire, heating up watery dal or commenting on the rottenness of the food was enough to be called to the gumti. Allegations of unnatural sex also drew the wrath of the authorities. False charges were made by their hangers-on with the intention of keeping people under their thumb.

In 1975, the barbarous torture inflicted upon inmates in solitary confinement was enough to make the cruelest of the inmates shudder with fear. Throughout the day one could hear the victims howling with pain. Even before the morning meal of dalia was given, they were beaten up. If out of sheer pain, the battered inmate delayed or hesitated to eat his dalia, he was thrashed again. With shaky hands and trembling fingers he would force the morsel of food into his mouth amidst convulsive sobs as tears dripped into his bowl. We got used to their howls and screams. Our sensitivity was almost dead. But we trembled to imagine the same fate befalling us.

Sometimes we chanced upon inmates who retained their spirit even in this torture chamber and refused to break down. Among them were Dayashankar and Santoshanand who had spent most of the thirteen years of their jail term in solitary confinement, with the continual accompaniment of torture. They would be let off every once in a while and then shoved in once again on some flimsy pretext or other. They never entered into brawls with any of the inmates. Once G.L. Gupta awarded three hundred blows to Dayashankar with a cane fashioned out of a green branch of neem. Dayashankar extended his left hand and the muscleman struck with all his might. A red gash appeared, cutting across his hand to his bare arm. The second blow fell on his stretched palm with the same force. Dayashankar turned his face away and endured the pain. Then the stinging blows fell on his hand in quick succession. Soon his arm and hand turned into a bloodied mess but Dayashankar refused to yield or change his hand. Superintendent Gupta then stopped the pakka and asked, "How many did you count?"

"Huzoor, one hundred and seventy-six," the pakka replied.

"No, you haven't counted correctly. Start again," Gupta barked.

The lashes started once again. But poor Dayashankar suffered all the blows on one hand and looked as if done to death.

His whole arm was soaked in blood. As the cane hit his hand with full force, blood splattered and sprayed all around. Fibres of flesh turned to pulp and flew into the air. By the time the counting was over, the white of the bones had become visible.

"Why didn't you turn over the other hand?" Gupta asked Dayashankar.

"To blast your ego, you sinner!" Dayashankar answered.

In response to this he was hung upside down from a tree and thrashed till his body was a mass of mangled flesh. Later he was given some first aid and sent off to his solitary cell. His hand never recovered as the bone had cracked.

Santoshanand was an educated young man. He protested against adulteration in rations provided to the prisoners and took it upon himself to expose the bada sahib's corruption. On the occasion of Gupta's sister's marriage, a lot of items made by prisoners such as beautiful rugs and carpets, garden umbrellas and wooden furniture, mosquito nets, colourful strings for cots, and flower vases were readied for the dowry. All the stuff had been loaded onto trucks which stood outside the superintendent's house the day of the send-off for the newlyweds. Santoshanand conspired to bring all the senior officials of the district to the jail for a crackdown. To attract their attention, he and two other prison inmates climbed a tree within the prison compound. At once the security sirens started blaring. The moment Gupta heard the commotion he quickly sent away the trucks and bid adieu to the bride without waiting for the marriage rituals to finish. Only when the magistrate reached the jail precincts did Santoshanand and his fellow conspirators get down from the tree, but their plan had suffered a blow due to Gupta's cunning. As expected, Santosh and his fellow-in-crime were thrown into solitary confinement and tortured beyond anybody's imagination.

When Gupta got his transfer orders he called together all the prisoners and told Santosh that he would be released from solitary confinement if he sought pardon. But bold and brave as he was, he refused to do so and spat with hatred. Only upon the arrival of the new sahib was he released from the solitary cell.

During this terrible period, I secretly wrote letters to my comrades. At times, the prisoners were given a postcard each to write to their dear ones, messages which were then strictly censored. One of my postcards fell into the hands of the jailor. It was placed before G.L. Gupta, and I was asked to appear before him. I hid the remaining secret papers and braced myself to be thrown into a solitary cell. It used to be commonplace in those days. I waited in great apprehension of being asked to appear before him but Superintendent Gupta never sent for me. Instead, my history ticket was stamped with the word FETTERS. This was an unbelievable incident of his tenure, for in the normal course my misdemeanour would have invited the harshest of punishments. I was put in fetters. By this time I had become so used to being in irons that I accepted the trouble without fuss. They remained on my legs to the end of Gupta's tenure.

11

The spectre of caste and one loud anti-brahmin

Legend has it that when the hungry mob encircled the palace of Louis XVI of France, the Queen, Marie Antoinette suggested innocently, 'If they don't have bread why can't they eat cake?' A similar story goes around in our village. A poor mother tried to pacify her daughter crying of hunger by saying that she would be married into a family where she would have all comforts—servants to wait upon her, expensive clothes to wear, lots of jewellery to put on and a doting husband. On hearing all this, the little girl saw her dream shatter, and looking at her mother with disappointment she asked, "But mother will I get bread to eat?" Between the two cases, one had never seen deprivation even in her dreams while the other had suffered deprivation to the extent that bread was the most precious of riches.

We were in a similar situation. If we got sufficient rotis to eat, it counted as a windfall gain. As was the usual practice in jails, rations were pilfered right at the godown and all the officials in the hierarchy had a fixed share in them. Once the rations reached the kitchen store, the warder took his cut.

Green vegetables produced in the jail were sold off and the money shared.

In the Fatehgarh jail, we were given a watery masur dal (red lentil). Some flour was added to make it thicker. Tiny worms floated in this concoction. We took them out and then dipped our rotis in it. I was disgusted to see inmates mash their rotis in this dal and eat it up nonchalantly. Once this stock of rotten dal was over, we were given rice for both meals during the cold months of December and January. I like rice but the kind we got here is hard to describe. It was difficult even to tell whether it was a handful of rotten boiled rice or a mashed gruel. Ants in the dalia were a common sight. One day as I was having my meal in the barrack, I found a piece of dried mango in the masur dal. In those days there were frequent power cuts and I couldn't quite make it out in the dim flickering light of the lamp. I soon realised that it wasn't a piece of mango I had been sucking on, but a dead cockroach. Sometimes, we had to eat just rotis and salt. In the name of vegetables, we got rotten smelly stuff unfit for consumption. As a result, most of the inmates suffered from serious stomach ailments. Diarrhoea and dysentery were common complaints. Batches of anaemic prisoners with pale, sickly faces would go to the hospital, from where they would be dismissed with some general pills or even spurious drugs while genuine medicines were secretly sold off by the doctors and compounders.

The prisoners who kneaded flour for bread were beaten

with a leather belt or broom to make them work harder. Kneading such large amounts often broke their fingers. They were beaten even after they became unconscious. When this work was given to a weaker inmate, he was a terrible mess, crying as he kneaded the flour in a cement trough with his feet. I could always hear the ongoing brawls and beatings that took place in the kitchen. Inmates who made rotis over the huge furnaces became dark in complexion because of constant exposure to heat. The dark skin stretched over cheek bones made their scorched faces look terrible. In this atmosphere of terror all prisoners had to cooperate in stealing rations from the kitchen.

While there is no provision in the jail rule book to delegate work on the basis of religion, caste or social status, the authorities did set work according to caste, owing to their brahmanical mindset. Cleaning duties were assigned to prisoners from the oppressed castes such as chamar, paasi, dhobi, dhanuk and such. Had there been a kamaan to wash clothes, prisoners of the traditional dhobi caste would have been assigned the job. An 'upper caste' man with any education at all would be taken up by the jailor or other officials as their peon, writer, or godaami (storekeeper). Not even illiterate prisoners of the dominant castes were employed in the safai kamaan (cleaning section); instead they were inducted into soot-katai (spinning) and dera kamaan (where massive military tents and other articles procured by the state were manufactured). A shrewd priest-type character was once interned at the Fatehgarh Central Jail. In the morning, after the counting was done, he brought flowers from the garden and, placing them on the jailor's table, told him with folded hands that he was a brahmin priest. He was assigned to the cleaning of the flower beds, and from that day on it became his daily ritual to bring flowers for the officials. Sometimes he would chant incoherent mantras and on special religious occasions tie the auspicious red thread or kalawa on the wrists of officials. Whenever he got the opportunity, he would preach during conversations and never lost a chance to show off his knowledge and wisdom. As for the job of tidying the flower beds, all the work was done by other inmates who came from backward castes or dalit communities.

So intricately was the caste-ridden structure of Indian society replicated in the prison system, it also informed the practice of corruption. At the Hardoi District Jail, a well-off brahmin prisoner was once assigned the duty of cleaning filth, simply so the jail authorities could extort money to relieve him of this shaming work. It proved an effective psychological weapon. He gave in, and a large amount was duly squeezed out of him. Extracting money from dalit and ordinary prisoners was routine, requiring no particular ingenuity. Their visitors had to bring money and that was that. There was even a fixed warder to collect it from them. Those poor dalit visitors who had nothing to give would somehow pool together a little money to get to visit the prisoners occasionally. The jail employees also exacted back-breaking work from dalits and no exceptions were made for age or infirmity. Amongst the most wretched of the prisoners, dalits predominated. The consciousness of caste was not merely a tacit suffusion in the workings of the jail. It could be passionately voiced too.

Gourishankar was popularly known as Gouriya. He was also called 'baggad' because he was a troublemaker, one who brawled at the slightest provocation. Gouriya was tall and very dark. He generally remained quiet and if he spoke to anyone it was mostly out of context and irrelevant. During summers he remained bare-bodied except for a pair of underpants. Being anti-brahmin was his greatest merit or demerit, which he expressed not through any argument but by his curses. Knowing his temperament, the brahmin inmates tried to avoid him rather than get into altercations. B.D. Sharma, the junior jailor of the circle, was himself a brahmin. The activities of Gouriya often reached his ears and he had devised a strategy to deal with him. Every six or seven days, he would summon Gouriya before the circle office. At one hollering from the jailor, Gouriya would immediately squat with his hands on his ears in the murga (rooster) position. The jailor would send for a lathi to beat him with, which made him run away in fear. This was not revenge for Gouriya's anti-brahmin attitude but to control and tame his baggad rants. One day when he was summoned for the murga punishment, he told the jailor, "Huzoor! Make me a different bird today." The jailor shooed him away by striking his lathi on the ground.

In our barrack, my berth was next to Gouriya's. He did

not generally talk nonsense with me, but at night he would babble stories from his past and tell wonderful tales of Basra and Baghdad, of military adventures and journeys at sea. I guessed that he was talking of the days of World War II when the British had recruited common villagers into the military. Gouriya may well have gone and signed up as a recruit. In the evening before the barracks were closed, he would fill my earthen pot with water, cover and keep it in the jhirri, the narrow space between two berths. I deliberately never thanked him for this.

Sometimes, lying on his back in the evenings, he would suddenly start cursing, "Damn these thread wearers! These goddamn tilak wearers!" But when Pandey-ji, the teacher and jail's writer, lying on the neighbouring berth, scolded him he would lie down quietly. Ramgopal Panda, whose berth was also close by, was rattled by these outbursts. Panda was an old man of sixty-five years, with a beard and moustaches. Occasionally, he found the time to worship. Whenever Panda-ji suffered from Gouriya-sickness, he would complain and share his pain with me. He belonged to a village called Naubatganj close to the river Ganga situated four to five kilometres away from Bangarmau. He was doing time for a murder in connection with a fight for supremacy among the pandas.

On a winter day, Panda-ji was sunning himself against the outer wall of the barrack. It was our day off work. A little away from Panda-ji stood Gouriya, also leaning against the wall. He had arranged his foot over the other leg in such a manner that his slipper faced Panda-ji. He continually shook his foot, looking intently at Panda-ji and then at his slippered foot. This went on for quite some time. In the end, Panda-ji left the compound in a huff to complain to the jailor. The jailor sent for Gouriya who said that he was only sunning himself against the barrack wall. He was summarily thrashed and kicked out. Upon returning, he sat among the prisoners out in the sun. His rumblings began once again, "May the sisters and daughters of these goddamned tilak wearers, these thread wearers be fucked!"

Till the end, I could not understand why Gouriya, an ahir by caste, was so revolted by the brahmins. Perhaps the brahmins had exploited someone from his village in the past. Whatever it was, he had certainly taken it to heart. He spoke not with the clarity of an ideological opponent, but a still more implacable personal hatred.

Holi, Eid, 26 January and 15 August were our biggest festivals. Not that we were great patriots, nationalists or true Muslims but because these occasions brought us good food and this meant more than anything to us. Although during the Janata regime in 1977, we got good food once a week, even tea once a day, in reality it was the prison officials and workers who benefitted more than the inmates. It became easier for them to steal tins of cooking oil and Dalda from the kitchen. The result was we got puris fried in little oil and halwa that was an apology for itself, cooked as it was in filthy-looking jaggery.

In 1975, I was extremely weak, frequently had blackouts and it became increasingly difficult for me to work. I was listless. Every other day I went to the hospital but there was nobody to listen to my problems. Ultimately, I confronted the chief medical officer knowing that this could land me in the solitary cell where, I thought, my likely death would at least end the suffering. To my surprise, the doctor admitted me. Within a week my condition got worse and I kept running a temperature. I could not walk, or even turn in bed. The doctor was regularly informed and he visited me every day. I felt death was approaching me. It turned out I had jaundice. During this time, Dr Gopal Gupta remained extremely sympathetic towards me. Multiple courses of injections continued, intravenous infusions of glucose were administered, and I recovered in five to six weeks. How can I ever repay the debt of the two prisoners from my own district, Siyaram Saini and Krishna Pal Singh, who nursed me back to health.

During my stay in hospital I discovered that of the many quintals of milk supplied for sick prisoners, more than half reached the homes of officials. The prisoners got a white watery liquid that passed for milk. Good medicines were stolen by the hospital staff. The contractors charged heavily for the rotten fruit supplied to the hospital. The hospital uniforms of prisoners and their bed sheets were changed only if a visit by a higher official was expected. The moment the official left the premises the clean clothes and bed sheets were taken away. Patients helplessly lay in their soiled beds and grimy clothing. The beds were infested with bugs that sucked patients' blood with the same dedication as the jail authorities.

A bald compounder with shifty eyes would set three to four litres of milk for curd. As soon as he arrived in the morning, his toadies made lassi for him. After having his lassi, he took a round of the hospital letting out streams of abuse on the patients. This happened a number of times in the day.

After I recovered, my mausi (my mother's sister, not my wife's mother whom I also called mausi) and my wife paid me a visit. At my wife's prodding, mausi told me that my wife was afraid that I may not like her taking up a job without my permission. A friend and comrade of mine, Ajay Sahgal, had a plastics factory in Kanpur that manufactured toys. Sahgal gave Dulari some light work there so she could earn her living. Sahgal's wife also respected and helped her. Ramdulari now lived with my mother at her brother's home in Kanpur. I was happy that she no longer had to depend on others for her basic needs.

My wife came to visit me at intervals of one or two months. She secretly carried all my letters and gave me news of the world outside. But the thought of her future worried me and made life harder.

12

The larger jail called Emergency

There was no library in jail where the prisoners could read books. Neither was there any private supply of newspapers. Each circle got a newspaper that went directly to the deputy jailor's office. After him, it reached the hands of a few privileged convicts—peon, writer, storekeeper. Some of the educated prisoners would occasionally get to read the paper, either outside the deputy jailor's office or at their barracks, thanks to the benevolence of the factotums mentioned above.

On the evening of 26 June 1975, when the prisoners returned to their circles from the factories, I asked a prisoner-peon from the jailor's office for the newspaper. I saw the bold headline of the Emergency on its front page, and the whole newspaper was full of related news. Curiously, the editorial column was blank with only the sign of a question mark that said a lot without saying anything. Hurriedly, I scanned the newspaper for all its headings and sub-headings. I was disturbed by a horde of troubling thoughts. Yet, there came to my subconscious mind a faint glimmer of hope on seeing the question mark in the editorial column. Man certainly finds a way to redeem his freedom of expression even in adversity, which may in future lead to complete liberation.

As far as I can recollect this was the *Dainik Jagaran*, a Hindi newspaper with a big circulation. Like other print media, its owner and journalists were also targeted by the Emergency regime. Yet, I was shocked to learn later that when Indira Gandhi visited Kanpur during the Emergency, Narendramohan Gupta, the editor of this very newspaper, was at the forefront to welcome her. (Later, he became close with the BJP leader L.K. Advani and was made a Rajya Sabha member.) As far as I can tell, to these followers of the Jan Sangh and RSS, the act of putting a question mark in the editorial was only a commercial strategy to increase circulation during these troubled times; apprehending future oppression, they found other ways to surrender before the Emergency.

The little hope I had preserved of release from prison now seemed futile. The circumstances under which the Emergency was declared made it look as though it might be prolonged endlessly, or if it was lifted at all, Indira Gandhi would by then have destroyed the democratic structure of the nation forever. Well-known leaders were being arrested. Frenzy and fear ran through the prison. It must be admitted that to those already there the Emergency made little difference, but prison is a place of rumours and widespread illiteracy. A lot of misleading stories began to circulate, such as that no one would be released by the courts now. Indira Gandhi would decide whom to release and whom not to. The most vicious rumour that went around eventually was that all prisoners would be sterilised.

The number of the imprisoned did swell as hundreds of political prisoners were thrown into the barracks of Fatehgarh Central Jail. The First and Second Semi-Circles were packed with these political prisoners. The Maintenance of Internal Security Act (MISA) had been invoked against many of them for political reasons. The number of prisoners rose to three thousand. Security was tightened and jail employees were instructed to be more vigilant. But Superintendent G.L. Gupta's dictatorial attitude could not subdue these prisoners of state. The new arrivals shouted earsplitting slogans of 'Bhujia ya tarkari hai, ya baillon ki hariyari hai?' (Is this food for humans or fodder for cattle?) And, 'Gupta teri tanashahi, nahi chalegi, nahi chalegi' (Gupta you're a crook, your tyranny won't be brooked), directed at the mismanagement and adulterated food.

The prisoners shuddered to hear G.L. Gupta thus challenged and thought that even if nothing else happens, baton blows were bound to fall on the leaders. These miserable inmates with their shattered self-esteem and dead souls believed Gupta to be the world's most powerful person. Decades of confinement had dimmed their perception. Despite Gupta's display of muscle power through a hundred baton-wielding nambardars and warders who followed him around, the deadlock could be resolved only through negotiation between the two groups. The inmates now realised that their bada sahib was not invincible after all.

The bada sahib's ceremonial procession drew ridicule from

the political prisoners. Whenever they found an opportune moment, they chanted in unison:

Bol jamure kya dekha?
Bina tilak ka raja dekha
Aur jamure kya dekha?
Chanwar dulate pakka dekha.

Tell me sidekick, what do you see?
An unanointed king is what I see.
What else, sidekick, do you see?
A muscleman waving a fly-whisk.

An infuriated bada sahib looked for an opportunity to crush their ego. Soon, he found it. One night, Pankaj, a MISA prisoner, had a pain in his chest. His friend, a young man of about twenty years, was giving him a body rub. As a result, the bed rocked. When a warder on duty peeped through the window grills to enquire, the youth told him the reason. But in order to be in the good books of Gupta, he raised a ruckus saying that the two were having unnatural sex.

Hearing this, all the MISA prisoners became infuriated. It was a noisy disturbed night. Early next morning, Pankaj was brought before the superintendent while the rest of the state prisoners were kept in lock-up. When Pankaj sat on a chair in front of Gupta, a ferocious-looking pakka knocked him off the chair with a tight slap. Gupta pretended to stop the pakka but the boy had been hit at his instructions. This incident created widespread discontent among the state prisoners. Immediately after this, Gupta had leaflets distributed among the inmates which read:

Bol jamure kya dekha?
Neta ke upar neta dekha.
Aur jamure kya dekha?
Machhardani hilte dekha.

Tell me sidekick, what did you see?
Saw one leader atop the other.
And sidckick, what else did you see?
Saw their quivering mosquito-net.

The prisoners chanted these words with great relish and ran around shouting them out. Who could tell these senseless creatures that it was all a lie, a fabrication. They just loved repeating "Bol jamure…" perhaps because this gave them the freedom to create a ruckus, by leave of their Great Master himself.

It was surprising to me that during the cold war between the prisoners of the Emergency and jail officials, the loyalties of the common prisoner lay with the cruel masters who had never treated him any better than a beast. Such prisoners, with the mindset of slaves, cursed the politicals and stole things from them to please their masters. It goes without saying that with the connivance of such people, protesters and political prisoners in our jail were frequently thrashed and the matter disposed of by reporting such incidents as common brawls. In our country, and perhaps all over the world, the structure of the prison system crushes the spirit of long-term ordinary prisoners to turn them into callous brutes, and that is the extent of their mental reform.

Many of the political prisoners and seditionists came from far-flung districts. They were brought here from jails close to their native place without their families being informed. They longed to see their families but rarely got to do so. The officials had been instructed not to allow them to write more than the stipulated number of letters, with every word monitored and censored.

During this time, the jailor of the First Circle was a drunkard, and a suspicious, cruel and cunning man. He showed concern for the state prisoners, but this was deceit. Impressed by his friendly behaviour, some MISA detainees sat and chatted with him believing that if they kept the jailor in good humour, they would be allowed to send more than one or two letters home. He even encouraged them to write more letters. By evening, when many letters collected on his table, he would hand them over to his peon and say, "Go and give them to 'Chirag Ali'."

This was code for them to be burnt behind an old deserted barrack while the inmates waited endlessly for letters from home that never arrived. Rajkumar the peon was a decent man. He felt terrible about burning the letters but had no other option. We were quite close to each other and occupied the same barrack. One day, after lock-up, he brought a packet of letters in his pocket which he couldn't burn. He confided in me about them. I could not help but read every single letter. Later we sealed them with a paste of jaggery and gram. These letters gave voice to deeply personal emotions. Having read them, I sat down and held my head in my arms in complete dejection.

The next day, my father was expected to arrive. I convinced Rajkumar to let me have these letters and carried them in a bag to my father. I requested him to post them in Kanpur. During family visits, and sometimes even before the visits, the inmates were thoroughly searched. Had those letters been found on me that would have certainly spelt my death. Later, with Rajkumar's help, I found other ways of smuggling out letters.

Prisoners managed to find ways to sneak in paper currency received from their visitors, despite strict vigilance and the high chance of being searched. The visitor followed the instructions of the inmate, who folded his gamchha (shoulder cloth) and placed it on the floor. While putting legitimate articles on the gamchha, the visitor slipped the contraband into its folds. At the end of visiting time a search of the prisoner's person and belongings was mandatory, but this could be a pretend exercise. The prisoner then carried his loot back to the barrack. Sometimes, visiting relatives would remove the tobacco from a few cigarettes and roll currency notes into their tubes. This was risky as any nambardar or pakka the prisoner encountered on the way back could extract a cigarette as toll.

Prisoners who had a pact with one of the warders collected the desired supplies through him once he had taken his own share. It was difficult to keep such money safe. The cash would be hidden in the gap between the bricks of one's berth and the gap closed over with mud. Others gave their money for safekeeping to authority figures among the inmates—such as a writer or peon to the jailor—with whom they shared good terms. These personages were seldom searched and could successfully conceal prohibited articles.

Meanwhile, the political prisoners had also established secret conduits. There were warders in their favour who carried information for them out of jail. The nature of these warders was very typical of their class. On the one hand, they thrashed all the prisoners, political or common; on the other, they cooperated with them on special occasions.

The internationally renowned book *Notes from the Gallows* by the Czech revolutionary Julius Fučík, written in pencil on tiny bits of paper during his incarceration in a solitary cell, was smuggled out of prison with the help of such a warder. During British rule in India, when the big leaders were put into prison, these warders played an important role as a communication link. No one will ever learn the name of the warder who smuggled out the autobiography of the great martyr Ram Prasad Bismil in installments from the Phansi Garad (the execution cell) of Gorakhpur jail. Many such noble souls also helped the MISA prisoners. My own experience was quite amazing. One of the warders did such a daring thing for me it would have cost him his job had he been discovered. He brought me a camera so I could shoot pictures to send home for remembrance. I kept the camera for two days, but did not find the opportunity or courage to use it. Had it been found on me, it would certainly have been construed as an attempt to map the prison and plan an escape, even a grand conspiracy. He did this for me out of the goodness of his heart and it is distressing that I cannot mention his name, much as I wish to. I had addressed him as 'Bhai sahib' and never learned his name.

Having remained the kingpin of Fatehgarh Central Jail for about six years, G.L. Gupta was transferred during the period of Emergency. Known to be the worst tyrant ever in the history of the prison, his departure was a relief to the inmates but the shadow of his terror remained for a few more months. The prisoners were apprehensive that he might return. Only after the new superintendent took over did the deathly silence gradually break. The new superintendent K.S. Pandey was a sensible man. He had concern for the prisoners. Corporal punishment and highhandedness continued but not directly from him. Consequently, the atmosphere of terror gradually waned.

Pandey-ji had the habit of picking his nose while talking.

I remembered that during 1967–68, when he was the jailor of Lucknow District Jail, I—then a student in Kanpur—was brought to his jail as a member of the state's United Opposition Front, arrested along with the hundreds who had protested before the Vidhan Sabha Bhavan. This was the first time I was arrested, and stayed in prison for a month. Among my fellow detainees were the communist leaders Shiv Kumar Mishra, Shankar Dayal Tiwari, R.N. Upadhyaya, Vijaypal Singh, Ramharsh Vidrohi, samajwadi (socialist) leaders Arjun Singh Bhadauria and Ramsevak Yadav, student leaders like Ram Asrey Verma and Surendra Singh, and 'the joker of Indian politics' Raj Narain.

Seeing the superintendent rubbing his nose after all these years evoked innumerable memories. There was a world of difference between prison life then and now. Then my ambition had run high. Confidence was at full steam. I had dreams in my eyes. I often reflected in solitude how my role in the socialist struggle would be significant. But these convictions were now dying as if on the gallows; as was I, serving my life term. Now I was reduced to a prisoner in a red striped vest, pajama and cap. I could see only red bricks around me, and each day seemed like a year.

The Emergency had made my life tougher. The reports in the newspapers made me fearful for my family. If I got no news of them for a long time, I would imagine that my brothers were arrested under the conspiracy-related provisions of MISA or my father was being interrogated by the CID. It felt as though all my loved ones—mother, father, brothers, wife—had been imprisoned in the larger jail called Emergency. Truly, the entire nation had turned into a prison. It was also known that thousands of labourers living on footpaths, in shanties and filthy areas of Kanpur had deserted the city, fearful of forced sterilisation and the threat of MISA.

Naxalite workers were being decimated in fake encounters. According to press reports, in the years 1970–76, in Andhra Pradesh alone one hundred and thirty-five men, women and children were killed for political reasons. Vempatapu Satyanarayana (known as Satyam) and Adibhatla Kailasam, both leaders of the Srikakulam peasant uprising of 1967, were shot dead. Telugu artists and poets, both men and women, Subbarao Panigrahi, Rameshchandra Sahu, Panchadi Nirmala, Gorakala Ankamma and Telakala Saraswati were shot dead. Twelve-year-old Pondooru Viraswami and Savara Ramu, who was seventeen, Dhananjay Rao and Prakash Beleru Umapati were also brutally killed by the police. Seventy-three-year-old Goda Gopana and sixty-year-old Penda Lingana were murdered in Khammam. Former members of the legislative council of Andhra Pradesh Neelam Ramachandraiah and student leader Jampala Prasad were shot dead in Vijayawada. Old Kolla Venkaiah was imprisoned and thrashed.

In West Bengal, during the regime of the Congress-led government of Siddhartha Shankar Ray, hundreds of young men were killed in Waranagar and Kashipur. Between the years 1970 and 1975, seventy-five prisoners were killed in various jails and many more were beaten up. Sixteen political prisoners were killed in Bhagalpur jail of Bihar on the charge of an attempted breakout. Gurcharan Singh, Kaku Singh and Deedar Singh of Manke village, which fell under the old police station of Bagaha of Faridkot district of Punjab, were murdered. As a result, twenty-five thousand farmers of Punjab protested in fury. The Punjab police even captured the eighty-two-year-old Bujha Singh, the senior-most revolutionary of Ghadar Party. He was shot dead on the bank of a canal. The son of the underground naxal worker Ramcharan was lured with a job and killed.

13

Of pimps, sexual abuse and honoured dacoits

Instances of sexual abuse of young prisoners are common in Indian prisons. Despite clear orders by the Supreme Court, state governments have been indifferent towards taking any steps to protect young prisoners. Till recently, conditions in Odisha were such that sixty-two prisons with a capacity of four thousand were crammed with six thousand prisoners each. Ten per cent of these prisoners were adolescent boys or young men. In 1982, the scale of abuse was so rampant in these overstuffed prisons that newspapers and other publications carried stories of it for days.

Over the long period of my imprisonment I saw that jail authorities and officials seemed to enjoy watching sexual perverts and listening to their tales. Some officials even acted as pimps. I know about a jailor who set up deals with prisoners, where, in exchange for money, he locked up the prisoner in a secluded room with the boy of his choice. The same jailor once took a good-looking young prisoner by the hand around the jail circle to auction him. That Punjabi lad cried all through the round. The jailor went on to be superintendent of a prison and became notorious as Gabbar Singh.

A lot of boys submit to a powerful prisoner thinking they would be safer under his protection. Resistance only adds the risk of being beaten up to that of abuse. During the reign of G.L. Gupta in Fatehgarh Central Jail, a fair-skinned handsome young boy of nineteen or twenty named Rashid was serving time. He was continually subjected to anal sex. Sometimes the pakkas who kept watch over him invited their prison guard allies and other pakkas to feast on him. After the tears of the first few days had dried, the lad endured the abuse mechanically, shattered by terror and violence. The depressed Rashid became so unhinged that he would at times go into paroxysms of laughter and howls.

One night there was a big commotion in Barrack Number 2 of our circle. Rashid and two other young men had consumed the seeds of the poisonous datura to end their life and escape this living hell. They did not die but became intoxicated and started jumping around and making a racket. All the prisoners of the circle woke up. That night the three were taken out of the barrack, beaten with wooden staffs and dragged to the infirmary. After being administered an antidote to counteract the toxic narcotic, they were locked in a solitary cell and beaten through the night. In the morning, pakkas were ordered to insert wooden rods inches into their rectums. Again, on the orders of the authorities in charge of the solitary cells, a torn leather shoe was dipped in water overnight and the boys were beaten with it first thing in the morning. In the day, the sequence was often repeated. This continued for days.

In the same jail, two inmate orderlies—confidants of G.L. Gupta—were notorious for abusing timid and good-looking boys. But no official or prison employee ever opposed them. They feared that if they took action against these tough inmates, their own corruption may be exposed. Among the juvenile prisoners are many who committed a crime in the heat of the moment, and others who fell into the bad company of dacoits. Serving long prison sentences, it is quite common for these boys to have no links left with their families. Shunned by all, and traumatised, if such a youth receives affection and acceptance from any person, he feels comforted and is often ready to submit unconditionally to him. In the immoral world of prisons this display of affection can find expression in the form of sexual abuse. Young prisoners become a substitute for women and gradually this compulsion turns into a habit or addiction.

Occasionally, enduring couples are formed. The identity of such pairs is an open secret, yet whether they find time for sexual intimacy or not is for them to know and others to wonder about. Even the jail authorities are aware of one or two such pairs. Unless it becomes too obvious, they are not restricted from seeing each other. In my time, the pair of Saheb Singh (who became a nambardar of the jail) and a boy called Halka had become quite well known.

There's a common saying in jail: To keep a boy is as expensive as maintaining an elephant. In light of this, it is rare to find a permanent couple. Generally, the workplaces of these pairs are different but they manage to have lunch and dinner together. They also look after each other. If one is shifted to another barrack, the other carries across the things he might need there and hands them over to his partner before the nightly lock-up. Such items may include ghee, sugar, pickle, and beedi-cigarettes brought in by visiting relatives, or some delicious food item smuggled in by a trusted warder.

The behaviour of other prisoners towards homosexuals, or those habituated to homosexuality, was matter of fact. However, no one spoke with them needlessly. If a prisoner showed too strong an inclination for boys, it was considered objectionable and others would pull his leg in conversation. In the code of ethics among prisoners, it is considered inappropriate to molest or win over another's special friend. In prison history there have been many cases of brawls breaking out because of interference by others. Murders were committed at the first chance. A long time ago an old-timer killed his unfaithful lover in the Fatehgarh Central Jail. This led to other similar incidents in the same barrack (number four). As a result, the barrack was declared accursed and shut down permanently. It remains closed even now.

It is a fact that open prisons are more effective and successful in reforming prisoners. Working in the open and breathing fresh air brings about change in the psychology of prisoners, and enables them to adopt a positive approach towards life. In 1960, with this view in mind, Babu Sampurnanand established the Sitarganj open jail (Sampurnanand Agricultural and Industrial Camp) in Nainital district. Spread across four and a half thousand acres in a deep forest, this agricultural farm allows prisoners closeness to nature as they work: the sight of flowing rivers, lakes and the red ball of the rising sun. At night, they retire to open barracks. They are granted parole for a few days every year so that they can spend some time at home with their families. Occasionally, the inmates are also allowed to spend three days with their visitors in a separate hut. Since its establishment, tens of thousands of prisoners on life term have been sent to this camp. The number of prisoners who escape from this facility is negligible. It is not surprising, therefore, that incidents of unnatural sex at this prison are generally unheard of.

But the aim of the political establishment is oppression, not reform. The idea of reform is tolerated only to the extent it would not infringe upon the establishment's class interest. We cannot even dream that naxalites like us would ever be sent to these open jails. For us it is thick iron doors, high walls, solitary confines and iron shackles and bars, because our aim is to destroy the hegemony of the oppressive bourgeoisie and replace it with the leadership of the oppressed masses of the proletariat. Yes, had we been dacoits from the Chambal it may have been possible for us to get facilities of all sorts.

In a separate quarter of the Fatehgarh Central Jail are housed dangerous dacoits who have surrendered. The main entrance to this part of prison is also independent. Many of these dacoits have been charged with scores of murders and robberies, for which they have been awarded life sentences. The Uttar Pradesh state government has classified them as 'baaghi' (insurgents) and made available to them facilities like open camps. Good quality food is provided to them. Each of them has been given subsidy for a buffalo. They supply milk to the prison and the profit is theirs to keep. They are given parole without any restrictions. In accordance with state policy, these dacoits, who have committed hundreds of heinous crimes, will be freed in a few years. But are they short of liberty in prison in any case?

When any function is organised in prison all of us are made to sit on the bare ground while the dacoits sit on chairs next to the officials. Despite serving life sentences, they are not made to wear the jail uniform like us. They wear clothes of their choice like free people. But this is no surprise in a country where only dacoits, politicians, civil servants and policemen are free. Officials of the state government pay them regular visits and through them establish communication with active dacoits. I have heard of how senior police officers came to the jail and took a few baaghi leaders out in jeeps for a day or two. Surely, such movements are not noted in any police records. As a result, these baaghis have become so bold that in January 1982 a dacoit, Desh Raj Singh, came out of jail and killed a trader in the town.

Dacoits are also permitted to keep their wives and children with them. The part of the jail in which they are housed is called Baaghi Sudhar (Reformatory for Rebels). Here liquor flows unabatedly. Under the pretense of being relatives, women are brought in for pleasure.

14

And my world fell apart

For those crushed under a life sentence, the wetness of tears or the dryness of words holds no meaning. Beyond the prison wall runs a long pitch road. The sound of vehicles hits the ears. From a distance, the cacophony of trains moving through the town's railway station and the whistles of engines being shunted print images on the subconscious mind. After a short halt, the engine spews its smoke and moves on.

Illness once again took me in its stranglehold. I caught typhoid. I was admitted to the prison hospital for one and a half months. I suspected I was falling prey to tuberculosis. The jail doctors were not able to come to a definite conclusion on my illness. I was sent to the Fatehgarh tuberculosis clinic to get an x-ray done. But no signs of TB were detected.

Of late I had started to get anxious about my wife. From the sick bed I wished my loved ones were with me. I wanted my wife to hold and comfort my sick body in her arms and touch my feverish forehead with her cool hands. Her sorrowful face floated before my eyes. It pierced my soul. I turned over in bed with great difficulty, and tried with trembling fingers to turn a page or two of the old magazine lying next to me. My eyes stopped at an advertisement where a beautiful healthy baby with outspread arms seemed to gurgle. The mother sitting nearby watched with love the strength and invisible power contained in those tiny fists…

For a long time I had received no word from my wife. My heart grew tired waiting endlessly for a letter. For us prisoners letters were the only medium to feel connected to the rest of the world. After a long wait I finally received one. But it did not have the same feeling as her previous ones. She seemed a lot more matter of fact. She did not show any particular interest in my illness. She wrote she would come soon to meet … that I should not worry … how else could a single woman cope… I could not understand the last bit.

At the meeting that ensued she looked stress-free and happy. She smiled at things I said. I wanted to know about my sister Devsena and about the elections in Kanpur. She told me that she had met Devsena recently but had nothing to say about the elections. I thought that she meant her inability to analyse the election situation. When I pressed for details she snapped, "Do I live for politics?" I felt as if I had fallen from the sky. My whole life was devoted to politics in its highest sense, and here was my life partner dismissing it. I could not have ever imagined this. After she left, her words rang for days in my ears. The clanging of the lock and iron bars morning and evening, the dull light of the lantern, the harsh calls of the guards and the regular beatings of the gong—all seemed as if making faces at me and mocking: Do I live for politics?

Our next meeting was about two months later. I melted the moment I was informed of the visit. I had been needlessly suspicious. It was nothing but my own frailty. There was no question of any fault in her. At the meeting she greeted me with her usual sweet smile. I smiled back. But it became clear very soon that she was forcing herself to be sweet. When the end of visiting hours was announced, she stood up without a moment's delay. My eyes fell on those who had come to visit other prisoners. How they longed to spend one more moment with their loved ones. It was particularly hard to get the women visitors to leave. When the visitors finally left, they kept glancing back at their imprisoned relative with a sad heart, till they turned the corner. They would even shout some forgotten message. But my wife, alas, had by now reached the main gate without even turning for a last look.

With heavy steps I walked back to my barrack. After some time, the prison's chief pakka, Mashuk Ali, who was posted at the prison gate came to me. He told me that an unknown person had come with my wife till the prison gate and both had left together. I was shocked. Many unanswered questions arose within me. Who was he? Why didn't he meet me? Why did my wife not say anything about him? Why did she say she had come by herself from Kanpur?

Eventually my mother and my younger brother in Kanpur also came to know about her affair. By now she had started living separately from my mother. After a month and a half or so, she came to visit me with my brother. She was aggressive and haughty. But suddenly she broke down, and as she left, promised me that such a thing would not happen again. But soon thereafter my brother saw her in a park with a stranger. Then without saying anything she left for her mother's home in Manjhiya. My father went to bring her back, but she refused to return. Instead she and her mother spread word in the village that I had left my wife.

In the meantime, my parole was approved by the state government. My wife and her mother also came to know of this. They tried their best that I should not be freed under any circumstances. My wife visited a colleague of mine in Lucknow jail, who held a grudge against me. He drafted a letter to the chief minister on behalf of Ramdulari, saying that I was a dangerous naxal and my release could lead to an eruption of violence. When the bail amount had already been paid and just a day or two remained for the release order to be received, my parole was cancelled on the basis of my wife's letter. Some newspapers splashed this all over.

The gentle beautiful village girl, whom I had loved from the bottom of my heart, had deserted me and gone to Delhi. Now there were two new names tattooed on her arms: Raj Kumari (perhaps her new name) and Trilok Singh.

15

The martyrdom of Shivnath

It was the extremely cold night of 23–24 January 1978. Wrapped in old and tattered blankets the prisoners slept as if lifeless. The loud calls of prison guards on their rounds shattered the silence of the night. I had not slept well in many days. Because of the endless wakefulness, my eyes were heavy with sleep, but they would droop for a moment and then open again. It was a strange restlessness—as if someone kept my eyes prised open. I tossed and turned, my face covered with the blanket. Suddenly, the footsteps of the guards became quicker and voices counting the prisoners rang out loud and clear. "All okay here, sir."

"Is Ramchandra Singh in this barrack?" a voice echoed from beyond the iron bars. I got up with a start. A torch in his hand, the guard was coming towards my berth. "Neta-ji (Leader sir), jailor sir is asking for you."

Wrapping a sheet around me I reached the iron grill. Jailor R.N. Singh stood there. Even after my greeting he remained silent, which was strange. My eyes rested on the face which was gripped in anxiety. The jailor spoke in a flat tone: "Shivnath Trivedi is no more."

I was stunned. I couldn't make out anything. I felt the blood was draining away from my body. Uttering a word or two of consolation, the jailor went away. Listlessly, I sat down with my back to the wall. The barrack guards and a few prisoners surrounded me. I was unable to make sense of their words of sympathy. Images of my great friend flashed across my mind one after the other. We had started our journey together in 1965 during the time of the naxal agitation. I had addressed the masses in Madho Ganj as a student representative. Seated on the dais was an ordinary-looking comrade to whom I was introduced. That he was in reality so remarkable had escaped me at the time.

Carrying bags full of revolutionary literature and ammunition, we travelled day and night like ghosts to far-flung rural pockets of Unnao and Hardoi. In some regions of Hardoi, Shivnath Trivedi's popularity was at its peak. People loved and respected him. His life was devoted to the cause of the oppressed masses. Poverty, troubles and danger were aplenty in his life, but he always remained a source of inspiration to us. He was that magic stone that turns iron into gold. He never knew to stop. He did not even look back.

Three months earlier he had said he did not want to live much longer like this. Despite serious health problems, he was not getting proper treatment. Along with diabetes, his stomach and intestines were in poor shape. But he was not admitted to the hospital until he couldn't walk. Only a short while before his death, when his condition turned serious, was he transferred from jail to the cantonment hospital, and was sent back to the jail hospital on 21 January. Even lying unconscious on a stretcher, he had thick iron shackles on his feet.

The state leader of the Naxal Protection and Release Society informed the independent legislator who was close to us and a few other people about Trivedi-ji's failing health. Nobody cared to speak up for the comrade who was fighting death. No one thought it necessary to request the jail superintendent and the concerned medical officers that Shivnath be sent to Kanpur Medical College or to ensure there was no negligence in his treatment. Later the legislator blatantly used the opportunity of Shivnath's death to his advantage by shedding crocodile tears in the legislative assembly.

On 24 January, when he was on his morning round, I requested Jail Superintendent K.S. Pandey to allow the comrades to visit the cantonment hospital with a police escort to see our dead friend one last time. At first this was rejected but keeping in mind the seriousness of the situation, the superintendent later agreed after consulting other officials. We were informed that his body was being brought to the jail and we should be ready. In about an hour and a half, all the comrades arrived from our respective circles and assembled in the central prison ground—silent like lost, weary and robbed travellers. Prison activities continued as usual, but the attitude of the staff and officials betrayed the awareness that something had indeed come to a cease.

Many a time, prisoners succumb to death within jail premises. From being victims of old age, to the shortage of medicine and lack of proper nourishment—and there are other reasons as well. These bodies are set afire at the Chirraya Taal—at a distance from the jail—by pouring kerosene oil on a pile of dry wood. On the way to the cremation, duty warders steal and send back to their own houses three-fourths of the wood and kerosene issued for cremating the bodies, while the half-burnt bodies are ripped apart and eaten up by vultures. It seems no one is disturbed by this.

But that day a strong force which could shake up all inertia had risen. This all-encompassing force has emerged at various times and places. It emerged forty-one years ago in this very prison as Manindra Nath Banerjee and today as Shivnath. It has no geopolitical boundaries. It could be Patrice Lumumba or Bobby Sands. It could be the damaged fingers and chopped-up body of Che Guevara lying in the forests of Bolivia. Sometimes it emerges as John Ball of fourteenth century Europe and Thomas More in the sixteenth century. It can be Chandra Shekhar Azad and Bhagat Singh of enslaved India and sometimes Kista Gaud and Bhumaiah of free India.

The hearse entered through the main gate of the prison. Warders and workers became busy getting the body down. We moved forward with trembling steps and offered help to the staff, but all strength had drained out of our hands. When one of the employees tried forcibly to straighten the stiff hand of the body, I cried out to restrain him as if Shivnath would feel the pain. The worker dropped the corpse's hand and gave me a strange look, as if I had gone crazy. Truly, it was madness. Shivnath wasn't there anymore.

As if we were culprits, we couldn't meet the eyes of his nephew who had accompanied the body. I stole a glance at him. A terrible revenge against the present establishment was raging in his eyes. I saw Shivnath in him. The body was placed near the fountain in the lawn. Prison staff and officers paid their silent homage. The jail superintendent arrived and took off his hat as a mark of respect. All the prisoners of the dera factory stopped work and came out. Hundreds of them in a line stepped forward one by one for a last glimpse of Trivedi. Very soon the body was covered with the flower offerings of the prisoners.

The moment came to take leave. Amar Singh, Vibhuti Prasad, Ram Raj, Badri Prasad and I offered the last homage. Laying the bunch of flowers stuffed in my shirt on the body, two drops of tears also fell on it. Palms folded in respect, I was overcome. All my materialism vanished, I don't know where. To whom was I paying respects? It was only a corpse, a dead body which would be destroyed very soon. Shivnath had left long back. His physical existence had long since ended.

Raj Bahadur and the senior warder, Surya Prakash Pathak, as a representative of the prison, accompanied the body. Pathak was close to us; he had a lot of affection for Shivnath. The next day he told me that the body was put in the freezing waters of the Ganga. As he described the scene, his voice choked with emotion. I could visualise the scene—the body of Shivnath wrapped in a red flag as a symbol of rebellion against the cruel regime of exploitation and oppression, moving up and down along the fast flowing waves of the Ganga. Moving on a long journey with the river, Shivnath was still giving a revolutionary message to the country.

16

When will the armour break?

During the naxal movement, two different approaches were adopted towards comrades imprisoned for long periods or on life imprisonment. One, the members outside might adopt the policy that the dead and those incarcerated for long periods were no longer the responsibility of the Party. Alternatively, their imprisonment may be treated as part of the revolutionary process, and the imprisoned comrades kept abreast of the latest political happenings and included in discussions on major issues. It should be obvious that only the former opinion was in play then. The state wing of CPI(ML) made no efforts to establish communication with the comrades behind bars. We had no idea if the Party had a presence left in Uttar Pradesh anymore. Later, we came to know that state leaders like Comrade Mahendra Singh—once the close confidant and trusted friend of Comrade Shivkumar Mishra—had plumbed the depths of ideological decline by breaking apart from the Party and setting up his own splinter organisation, called the Centre Team.

We did not even know if revolutionary forces were active at the national level or not. Nor did we know the ideological differences that had crept in among the national leaders of the Party. In the meantime, we got a copy of a press release issued by certain important leaders of the Party in which the campaign to eliminate class enemies was renounced and stress was laid on building a broader base of followers. All the comrades incarcerated in Fatehgarh jail completely agreed with the central premise of this statement, but we were sad and surprised that we had received the copy not from our comrades but the government. We were told if we gave a written undertaking that we accept this statement the government would consider our release.

We failed to understand why the Party was giving an opportunity to the government to use this statement of policy as a condition for our release. Still, presuming it to be the decision of the central committee and keeping in mind the discipline of the Party we gave written declarations in favour of the statement. Later we came to know that the the Party statement was passed on to the government by Comrade S.N. Singh without the permission or knowledge of the central committee. The most painful part was that amidst this misunderstanding, despite our written declarations following the government's wishes, the administration turned a deaf ear to the matter of our release.

The demand for the release of naxalite prisoners had begun a long time back. In North India, for the first time the brave and bold comrades of the Akhil Bhartiya Krantikari Yuva Morcha (All-India Revolutionary Youth Brigade) under the leadership of Ram Asrey Verma raised their voice through the organisation's mouthpiece *Yuvanak*. As a result of these early efforts, a national conference was held at Delhi on 20–21 April 1973 in which almost three hundred intellectuals across the country participated. Of them, R.K. Garg, Ratan Das, Dr Gyanchandra, Bodhayan Chattopadhyay, Arjun Arora, Bhupesh Gupta, P.C. Joshi, Jayashree Rana, George Fernandes and V.K. Krishna Menon were among the important ones.

At the conference, when senior leaders of the CPI were asked to put pressure on their party's government in Kerala to initiate the process of release of naxalite political prisoners in the state, they maintained a stoic silence.

After this conference, Protection-Release Committees were constituted in most states. In Uttar Pradesh one such committee was constituted on 9 June 1973, in which the role played by Dr Shabbar Hussain, C.B. Singh and Avtar Singh 'Bahar' was significant. Processions and demonstrations were held in various districts and towns for our release.

In January 1977, after the Emergency was lifted, the demand for the release of naxalite prisoners once again gathered momentum across the country. Under the aegis of the Uttar Pradesh Citizens' Freedom and Human Rights Committee, a seminar was organised in the Students' Union Building of Lucknow University on 1 October 1977, where representatives of different ideological groups participated and supported this demand. Efforts were made in different towns of the state to draw the attention of the new government to this issue. But the Janata Party government, like with other electoral promises in its manifesto, reneged on the promise of freeing naxalites. The faint hope generated by the change of government petered out.

Munni's betrayal and Shivnath's martyrdom had already broken me deep inside. In this state of half madness born of great disappointment, I don't mind admitting that my whole materialist outlook deserted me for a while and I even leaned towards spirituality and theism. In my derangement, I wanted to scream and cry, pull out my hair and tear off my clothes. Many times I thought of taking my life, but in the absence of means and opportunity the idea got shelved.

It was during this time that all prisoners in India undergoing life imprisonment suffered a major blow. We came to know that a new law had been promulgated by adding a new section—433-A—to the Code of Criminal Procedure (CrPC), so that the release of life prisoners would not be considered before completing the full fourteen years of incarceration. Before this the provision of release on probation after completing five years was in place, though it was a different matter that this provision was not implemented fully. Even so, a prisoner would generally be freed for good behavior in eight to ten years. To oppose section 433-A, prisoners across the state stopped work. Thousands of prisoners petitioned the Supreme Court through the superintendent. To understand the intricacies of this problem many prisoners often surrounded me.

A mass hunger strike was launched in Fatehgarh Central Jail protesting the 433-A issue. It originated in the Second Circle. Prisoners refused to leave their cells and go to their workplace in the jail, and they refused food. Many prisoners were put in solitary confinement. The next day a similar outburst was anticipated in the First Circle. Some leaders in prison were shackled and put in solitary confinement even before the morning prayers. On receiving this news, the prisoners assembled in the prayer ground became apprehensive and returned to work in the factory. The expected outburst was thus averted. After this frantic activity, officials brought the situation under control. Later thousands of prisoners submitted writs to the Supreme Court challenging this black law.

A few days on, my comrades and I submitted notice of a hunger strike to the government, demanding to be placed in a higher category. But the response of state minister Mohan Singh made us give up the stir. In his opinion putting the call for hunger strike on hold would create favourable conditions for talks with the government regarding our demands. Representatives of the Protection-Release Committee kept meeting Mohan Singh and Chhotelal Yadav, both ministers in the coalition government that ruled UP, in this regard. As a result of their efforts an order to grant a higher category to naxalites was passed, but thanks to bureaucratic manipulations this order could not be implemented. I got my writ as well as those of my friends registered in the high court. We were transferred to the Lucknow jail for our hearings. I was sent there in September 1980.

17

Between two worlds

At the Lucknow jail I was kept in a solitary cell. During the day, my room remained open and I was free to move around in the premises as and when needed. Our other comrades Amar Singh, Vibhuti Prasad, Badri Prasad and Ram Raj were lodged in the B class barracks. Their challan had reached here sometime before my arrival. The high court had already started hearing their writs and passed interim orders for them to be moved to a higher category. I spent most of my time with these comrades.

The solitary cells of the Lucknow jail were especially frightening and dark. There was only a small hole in the tin-fitted door of the cell through which one could look in or out. I started taking stock of the prisoners in solitary confinement. One or two were mentally deranged. A couple of them were perverts. In one cell was a middle-aged man and one-time prison absconder. Broad of jaw, tall in build, with cruel eyes, a hard voice, a beard like a maulvi, and a salt-and-pepper moustache. A terrible personality. He was usually let free during daytime. He cursed other inmates and officials and yelled over the most trivial things. All the inmates in solitary confinement were afraid of him. In the afternoons he summoned a fifteen-year-old juvenile prisoner, Ramsevak, to his cell, got him to clean the premises and press his legs as he showered him with abuses and kicked and punched him. Ramsevak often ran screaming from the cell but the pervert, cursing all the way, would steer him back in. Ramsevak was beaten up like this every day. I was surprised that the warder sided with that horrid prisoner and threatened the boy if he complained at all.

One afternoon, hearing Ramsevak's screams and shouts, when I tried to peep in through the half-closed door the man started cursing me. When I gave it back to him, he became quiet and threw Ramsevak out his room. Later, for as long as I was there, he stared at me angrily to cow me down, but from that day on Ramsevak's beatings stopped.

The same solitary confinement block held a juvenile prisoner, Girish. He was a good-looking boy and came from a good family. When out of his mind he would take off his clothes, shout and jump around and challenge anyone who came before him. For some reason he was always well-mannered with me. After a while he became normal and was released.

One day an inmate in the cell opposite mine was beaten badly. I could hear him sobbing. After thrashing him for long, when the warders emerged from the dark cell they hesitated when they saw me. One of them spoke: "Oh, he's a true rogue. I have plucked off his moustaches." The tales of solitary confinement remained the same, even away from the terror of the superintendent of Fatehgarh Central Jail and its unending naked dance of brutality.

Within the confines of the solitary enclosures, a platform was constructed around the neem tree. It had a tiny shrine of old bricks fixed with mud in which were kept some uncarved round stones. Prisoners had told me with great respect that this shrine had been made by Satyapal baba. Satyapal baba was none other than my co-accused Satyapal. He had been transferred from this prison to the Lucknow Adarsh Jail. I was amused at the irony that the comrade who had objected to my father's anointing my forehead on the day of our verdict eight years ago, was himself a baba now, a holy man. Not only this. Sham that he was, Satyapal baba had played a clever move. On the one hand, he sought cooperation from certain institutions in the name of naxalism; on the other, he spoke with CPI leaders showing his inclination to join their party.

This was not surprising. At the beginning of any movement there are a few anomalies because of which hostile elements also enter the system. During the initial days of the naxal movement, some people became members who remained revolutionaries only as long as their vested interests were not under threat. It's easy to acquire a special status among thousands of prisoners through prayers and rituals and become a sadhu but it's difficult to sustain your revolutionary consciousness. In the naxalite movement unscrupulous elements also flourished along with heroism. But these anomalies disappeared with time as the rot in the party was identified and attacked. Otherwise, apart from a few exceptions like Satyapal baba most of our comrades imprisoned in Uttar Pradesh tested true on the touchstone of revolution.

By now I had made several appearances in the Lucknow High Court. I had not been granted a higher category so far. An interim order was expected in this regard. But before my next court appearance, the senior superintendent—while on his rounds one day—informed me that the Supreme Court had accepted my writ against article 433-A and had granted bail. I was to be freed the next day. I couldn't believe my ears. I was speechless. What I hadn't even imagined was coming true. In fact, the Supreme Court had ordered bail on the writs against article 433-A submitted by thousands of prisoners till such time as a final decision was taken on the issue.

Till I was actually free, I fretted that a new hurdle might crop up. I did not have any change of clothes except the prison uniform. An undertrial prisoner arranged for a shirt and pair of trousers for me. After coming out of the prison gates, I looked back once and then walked towards Char Bagh. This experience was so unbelievable that I turned back many times thinking it might be a mistake, and imagined jail authorities running after me. But nothing like that happened. It is difficult to convey what a joyful experience it was to breathe this air of freedom under an open sky. It was evening when I caught a train to Kanpur. The first thought was to meet my mother. The train ran speedily. Sitting near a window, I was wandering free in a distant dream world.

I got the opportunity to stay out on bail for almost a year. During this period, I met many forgotten friends. I even searched for Ramdulari and found her in Delhi. I had received unconfirmed information that she now lived in Lakshmi Nagar under the alias Kamlesh. In a city like Delhi it is next to impossible to track down someone with only their name and locality to go by. With the help of a local friend I went through the registers of many government ration shops in Lakshmi Nagar. After a lot of hard work, I found her name and address. I knew she would have got the ration card made out in her name, since her cunning lover did not live in Delhi with her. He had a wife and worked in Kanpur. He had kept Ramdulari in Delhi as his mistress and visited her once a month or so.

On reaching her house, I called out her name. She was sitting on the lower parapet of the terrace. On hearing my voice, she got up startled. She carried a newborn in her arms. This meeting seemed like a strange dream at the time. For a moment, she looked at me, eyes wide with surprise. Then she almost fainted and was about to fall down but balanced herself. Clutching the baby in her lap, she sat down heavily. Her mother was with her. She took me into the room. After a while Ramdulari came down from the terrace and sat in a corner. I stayed there for some time. Both of us were silent.

What was there to say? She held out the child to me. The baby was very sweet, a daughter. I took her in my lap and looked at her. Two drops of tears fell on her little cheek. Handing the baby to her mother, I came out wiping my eyes and bought a doll from a nearby shop. Then I kissed the baby and left. Later, when I came to know that the child had died in a fire, I cried uncontrollably in my solitude. I never discussed this incident with my family or even my closest friends.

In the meantime, Shiv Kumar Mishra-ji, though he had retired from active politics, worked untiringly to secure full release for me and my other naxalite friends on the grounds of probation. He was joined in these efforts by the young and enthusiastic Kanpur leader, Comrade Purushottam Sharma. On the completion of the parole period in November 1981, I presented myself at the Hardoi District Jail. Then the challan was sent to Fatehgarh. We were told that within six months, a decision would be taken on the writs against article 433-A. Dreams now stirred in the eyes of thousands of prisoners.

18

29 September 1983

While I was out on bail, a massive strike was observed by the prison employees of the state. Since the British period, this was the only department that had never gone on strike. A jail association had been instituted in 1922 which till now had dealt with problems only on paper. For the first time, on 27 June 1981, the association decided in Lucknow to kick-start a widespread agitation. Soon thereafter, the government was handed a twenty-point demand letter in which besides compensation parity with the police department, provisions for accommodation, education and uniform were also stressed. From 8–15 July 1981, a public awareness week was conducted. Black armbands were worn as a sign of protest from 16–31 July. When the government failed to provide any assurance, around five thousand prison officers and workers across the state proceeded to strike on 10 October 1981.

In the years after the so-called independence of 1947, most of the people who now occupied government positions had done time in jail. It goes without saying that during British rule the jail officials, given their mental servility, had often manhandled and beaten up freedom fighters. The new rulers probably held this against them for a long time. It is no surprise that the various development programmes instituted for the public ignored employees working in various prisons. Suffering from guilt and low self-esteem, the jail officials themselves could not muster the courage to step forward and present their problems. Later, when the demands of prison employees were taken into consideration, the living standards of employees of other departments had risen. As a result, the facilities provided to prison officials and workers were way behind in comparison to other departments. This further aggravated their frustration. In order to counter the privations of their life, jail employees felt compelled to steal bread meant for prisoners or even extort a few rupees from female visitors coming from villages. With this mindset and attitude, they remained as cruel as ever towards the prisoners. As a result, prison employees never had a favourable reputation among the public or the prisoners.

Despite this, the prisoners' sympathies before the strike were completely with the jail employees. It was assumed that the prisoners would display symbolic acts of protest in support of the prison employees, so that the government was compelled to accept their demands. But on the eve of the strike, the jail employees jumbled up all prison keys and filled the keyholes with mud. They even poured kerosene into the porridge meant for the prisoners' breakfast and mixed saw dust in sacks of wheat flour. All this was done with the intention of creating disturbance in the prison: the prison could not open at the scheduled time, and the contaminated food provoked the prisoners. This was a foolish act, for it boomeranged on them. In the morning when the prisoners came to know the actual state of affairs, they flared up against the prison officials instead of the government. In retaliation, they gave their full cooperation and support to the Home Guard jawans who were looking after the prisons and to the officials of other departments posted there. In return, the prisoners were treated humanely. During this period, the prisons received full rations of better quality, prisoners were spared unnecessary discipline and punishment, and no facilities were curtailed. At some places, the prisoners were asked to use batons to control the striking prison employees locked up in cells who were creating a furore.

Therefore, despite the participation of ninety-nine per cent of the workforce the jail employees' protest did not yield the expected results. After a few days, they returned to work. But the after-effects of this strike lingered in the prison atmosphere for a long time. The jail officials who returned to work, especially the kingpins—around four thousand warders in number—became the staunchest enemies of the prisoners.

I arrived in Hardoi jail once again during this period of cold war and stayed there for almost a month. Comrade Amar Singh and Comrade Badri Prasad had also arrived. Later our challan was sent to the Fatehgarh Central Jail. At Fatehgarh too, the relations between prisoners and officials were hostile. The tactics of the employees showing off their power, attacking the barracks in the name of conducting searches and beating up prisoners without any reason had become a regular feature. In the meantime, I was housed in the Second Circle and assigned the job of unravelling cotton thread. I used to sit on a blanket and work quietly. Jailor Harnam Singh was an overzealous stickler for the rules and a man of irritable disposition. Prisoners, in general, did not have a good opinion of him. Even I had many skirmishes with him.

During this time, hope and despair played on the minds of many life-term prisoners. The timeline decided by the Supreme Court to consider the release of the prisoners entitled for probation had long since expired. The government extended the deadline for decision-making a number of times, and in some cases during this period release was postponed by many years. In retaliation, the prisoners of Bareilly Central Jail stopped work. This affected other jails of the state as well. The government was already annoyed by the submission of writs to the Supreme Court by life prisoners. This new circumstance added fuel to the fire.

One day in January 1982, we came to know that firing had taken place at the Bareilly Central Jail and five prisoners had been killed. The story in circulation was that the prisoners were trying to escape after breaking the main gate of the jail and had also attempted to kill the jail superintendent. This created quite a sensation in the Fatehgarh jail. The prisoners knew that the Bareilly incident was actually a well-planned conspiracy. Some days later, a few prisoners from the Bareilly jail were transferred to Fatehgarh Central Jail. Most of them had broken bones and were badly wounded. They were locked up in the solitary cells. In the bitter cold of the winter, they were left with a tattered blanket or two for days together.

Months later, when a couple of these prisoners were released from solitary confinement, it emerged that the prisoners' refusal to work at Bareilly jail had made an impact on other prisoners in the state. Hence, the senior officials decided to teach them a lesson. The then superintendent of Bareilly jail, Udit Narayan Singh, was considered to be a liberal. He was transferred out.

When the new superintendent Pundir took over, in a preplanned move he had all the belongings of the prisoners removed a day before. He asked them to assemble at one place and addressed them in a Hitler-like manner. When a prisoner stood up with his request, he was shot dead. There was commotion among the prisoners who ran for cover and hid themselves in the barracks. A lathi charge in the barracks followed soon thereafter. The solitary cells were opened and the prisoners were thrashed. Five prisoners were killed. Among them was one pakka, Dori Lal, who was pulled out from the barrack and shot at point-blank range as two warders held his arms. Later, a window in the superintendent's office was deliberately smashed and a story concocted that Pundir had had to escape through it to save his life.

For months together, the prisoners of Bareilly jail were subjected to cruel torture on a regular basis. Our three friends, comrades Kishan Lal, Baijnath and Chhotelal were also incarcerated in Bareilly. They were in separate lock-ups and hence were spared. The Bareilly firing had spread such terror that any prisoner trembled at the mere thought of filing a writ in the Supreme Court. Any prisoner who dared file a writ would be thrown into the living hell of solitary confinement at the slightest pretext. For almost a year the same condition prevailed.

In January 1983, I received a letter from Comrade Rakesh Dwivedi at Allahabad informing me that I had been awarded a higher category by the high court. A copy of the order accompanied the letter. The same month I was transferred to the Faizabad District Jail. Here I met the former jailor of Fatehgarh jail, Ram Naresh Pandey, whom I had known earlier. I have rarely come across a jail official like him. It was a marvel to me that he maintained a spotless reputation despite living and working within the evil prison system.

The higher category barrack where I was put up and its surrounding area were so spacious that we played volleyball there. The many-time MP of BJP Brij Bhushan Sharan Singh (who was young at the time) and Baba Gopal Das (who was associated with the Hanuman Garhi temple of Ayodhya) also participated in our games. Brij Bhushan Sharan Singh had been jailed in connection with taking cartridges from a mafia don of Eastern UP. This incident took place in connection with the tender for a theka (government contract) near Tarang cinema in Faizabad. Baba Gopal Das was a young mahant then, jailed in connection with some issue concerning the assets of the mahants of Ayodhya—a matter that frequently led to armed demonstrations, shooting and other skirmishes. (The violent jostling for assets among the mahants of Ayodhya and its anarchic fallout would call for another book.)

The personality of Baba Gopal Das and his reticence had impressed me. Brij Bhushan Sharan Singh and I often chatted while sitting atop a water tank. I can still remember him reciting his poem on the plight of the poverty-stricken victims of a heavy flood. It gave me a glimpse of his hidden strain of deep sensitivity.

I had an appeal filed in the Supreme Court to be released on probation. On the same matter, Comrade Rakesh Dwivedi had filed an appeal in the high court for me and our other friends. The high court accepted all the appeals and passed the order for release. The Supreme Court too passed the order of bail on my appeal. Eventually, I was released from the Faizabad jail on 29 September 1983. Other comrades too were released on bail one by one. In the meantime, the government was compelled to consider release on probation. Eventually my probation was accepted.

Upon my release, I headed to Kanpur. My mother was there. It was night when I called out to my sick mother who was in bed. She got up with a start. For a few moments she stared at me blank and speechless. On hearing my voice again, she took me in her arms.

> Your eyes are
> a rising ocean of pain
> Let us change this world
> as soon as we can!
> — Gorakh Pandey

After-Stories:
Conversations in Bangarmau

Interview with S. Anand

20 January 2017

On 2 December 2016, a Friday morning, I received an email from Madhu Singh, then a stranger to me, saying she had translated a naxal jail diary, *Thehre Hue Terah Saal*, written in Hindi during the Emergency years (1975–77) by Ramchandra Singh, a man from a working-class, 'Backward Caste' background of Bangarmau village in Unnao district. Bangarmau is some sixty kilometres from the capital Lucknow with its eponymous university where Madhu teaches in the Department of English and Modern European Languages. She underscored the significance of this text in five neatly listed points, each driving itself home firmly and clearly. I was riveted. I asked for the manuscript and a synopsis.

Slow reader that I am, I read the slim manuscript over the weekend and found myself wholly in its grip. I was in the presence of not just an absorbing story but of a natural storyteller who knew his craft. A strange and sudden burden was placed upon me: the burden that a true story told well places upon us all. Should we, and can we, look for *art* in a prison diary? What if it is not just a tale of suffering, but the story of resistance, of the quiet resolve with which the spirit fights back even when the body is broken, time and again? Is it okay to look for and appreciate art here, and to wonder at the aesthetic? Is it akin to falling in love while in pursuit of the revolution?

Ramchandra Singh falls in love with the adolescent Munni of Manjhiya village who, every time she 'emerged laughing from the emerald and yellow mustard field, the tiny yellow flowers clinging to her hair made her look like a pretty forest nymph'; Munni who then turns up as the 'graceful' Ramdulari after Ramchandra lands in prison; Ramdulari, who has now moved from village to town, whose 'taste' he tries to 'refine' and hence 'motivates her to read', to become a *comrade* in love. And Ramchandra says, with the pride that belongs equally to love and love of revolution: 'Within a short time, she imbibed a lot, and soon read Maxim Gorky's *Mother.* She liked the character of Powell very much.' What is the *taste* that needs *refinement* as Ramchandra-ji seems to think? Out of prison, when Ramchandra goes looking for Ramdulari in Delhi, she has become Kamlesh. What is the judgement we all exercise upon what we love? Why and how does Ramchandra Singh write with such a keen sense of language (a grace that Madhu Singh casually captures in English)? It is this artless-seeming art of Ramchandra Singh that drew me in.

After reading the memoir, I felt the need to meet him, to know more, at least a little more about this life of insurrection. What had happened before Ramchandra Singh landed in prison? What had happened after he got out? How is he now and what does he do? What does he think of our exhuming this story published variously in 1984 and 1991, in Hindi? In her email, Madhu Singh had quoted from one of the interviews she conducted with Ramchandra Singh in Lucknow: 'My jail diary is not for self-glorification; rather it should be treated as a symbol of longing and desire of the youth to find a way out of missed opportunities and unemployment despite big claims of progress and development.' Madhu had presented a paper on Ramchandra Singh's book and life at a conference at the University of Chicago at Madison in October 2016. A scholar there had suggested that she try and publish this book with Navayana.

What was Ramchandra Singh's crime? Inspired by the ideals of communism and the cry for an end to feudal oppression, Ramchandra Singh becomes a 'party *bachcha*', a party boy, when he is about 14, in grade 8. This is around 1960–61. He becomes an active member of CPI(M). At a young age, he becomes a member of the party's district committee. Naxalbari—India's 1968—happens in 1967. In 1970, he participates in a twelve-man attack on an oppressor landlord who terrorised the poor and the peasants under his thrall. This was in response to the 'annihilation of class enemy' campaign called for by Charu Mazumdar, inspired by Mao's call in China. The landlord, from village Bakhaura some fifteen kilometres from Bangarmau, was *annihilated*, to use the term Ramchandra Singh prefers. Many members of the squad were easily nabbed and put behind bars. Ramchandra Singh was one of them.

He was about 21, his *moustache still nonexistent*, as he says in the memoir. He begins to think about how he landed where he had. He decides to tell his story while yet in prison, and sneaks his manuscript out with the Party's help. It is a powerful story, about the dream of revolution and the love that awaits, and the love that betrays. He tells all this in spare prose, with long pauses and quick turns.

Ramchandra-ji started writing the jail diary around 1975 during a thirteen-year term (1970–83) served across five jails of Uttar Pradesh. This came to be serialised, with some additions, in 1984 in *Shaan-e-Sahara*, a weekly that's often described as 'progressive'—a wink of a term that means broadly Left and with a literary bent, the kind of magazine that has become tough to find now. In the 1970s and 1980s, in pre-liberalisation India, this weekend newspaper published from Lucknow enjoyed a good circulation and had been launched by the Sahara group (what is today the notorious Subroto Roy-led empire of nepotism and corruption).

Madhu Singh had explained in her email: 'A local Hindi journal, now defunct, *Samkaleen Dastavez*, edited by Prashant Kumar, republished it in a special issue (Vol. 2, Year 1, May 1991).' Titled *Thehre Hue Terah Saal* [Thirteen years at a standstill], the issue was dedicated exclusively to Ramchandra Singh's memoir and featured specially commissioned illustrations. Madhu had picked up a copy of this sometime in 2014 at a bookshop that Prashant Kumar now runs in Lucknow. *Samkaleen Dastavez* [Contemporary Dossier] had survived but a few years. Madhu got in touch with Ramchandra Singh through Kumar and sought his permission to translate the work. Given the current political climate and the easy persecution of anyone associated with naxalism or Maoism, some publishers were quick to reject the proposal without even reading it. It made the rounds till it reached me.

When I expressed the desire to meet Ramchandra Singh, Madhu Singh facilitated a meeting quickly. Ahead of this, Madhu and I met on 13 December in Delhi at my office, and as we shared our excitement over the manuscript we mapped the possible road ahead with Ramchandra-ji's involvement. Madhu purchased some Navayana books. I soon had a long telephonic chat with Ramchandra Singh.

On 19 January 2017, I took an overnight train to Lucknow. After breakfast at Madhu's apartment, with a hired hand driving my host's car, we passed Mayawati's massive walled enclosure of monuments to various anti-caste icons including herself. We soon hit a newly laid highway in the poll-bound state; this helped us traverse the sixty kilometres in under an hour. On the way, we shared stories about our lives and work.

This was also Madhu's first visit to Ramchandra Singh's house. We reached the village by noon. It was a warm and sunny winter day. It took us a while to find the Mohalla

Ghoorey Tola. The large village of Bangarmau has a population of some 45,000 comprising every caste in the graded spectrum from brahmin to the most oppressed dalit, and with a sizeable Muslim population pegged at 45 per cent in the 2011 Census. Most houses were of bare bricks put together loosely with hardly any cement. Few homes in this qasbah seemed able to afford a cement finish or tiles. Walking about the place that evening, conspicuous as an outsider, I saw that most Hindu houses had 'Sita Ram' graffitied on their walls. The handiwork, Ramchandra-ji would later tell me, of the far-right Rashtriya Swayamsevak Sangh and various affiliates of the Bharatiya Janata Party. I also saw the setting sun fall upon a brick wall where a hakim offered a boosted sperm count. Men went to relieve themselves in the privacy of a small patch of eucalyptus trees at one end. A drunk was shouting in the street that anyone who gave a dowry to get his daughter wed was actually paying a stranger to rape their daughter. It made sense. Many muezzins called the azan all at once as temples blared out bhajans in competition. The highway, marking 'development', rimmed one end of the qasbah. You could both see and hear the intermittent traffic. An open drain flowed along the narrow streets of the entire village. Young men whizzed by on bikes at high speed, their thumbs pressed on the horn. Robust pigs, rafts of clumsy ducks, goats wearing coats, docile cows and snarling dogs foraged the streets. Garbage and sewage often fused. The caste system's division of labour being more a division of labourers—as Ambedkar regarded it—was fully at work here. The scavenging castes, whose habitation was disparagingly referred to as Bhangiaana, was in its corner. It was their job to clean, and up to others to leave a mess right outside their homes. This, perhaps, was the quintessential North Indian village of the Gangetic plains.

Ramchandra Singh's home was modest. A small verandah with a wash area fronted the living room in which the sofa set occupied most of the space. A table was laid in the middle, where tea, warm drinking water, and meals would be served by the wife and daughter-in-law who'd soon be introduced. There were stacks of papers all around. In the 12 x 12 feet space, a cement rack affixed end-to-end along a wall held various books: progressive literature, history books, pamphlets, reports of party congresses, old journals. I presented him with a set of Navayana books, including Angela Davis' *Are Prisons Obsolete?* Ramchandra-ji immediately expressed interest in the tract by the feminist philosopher and former Black Panther who had once been imprisoned. Davis had twice run for the American vice-presidency on the Communist Party ticket during the Reagan era. He would, in a couple of weeks, call me having read this and Ambedkar's *Annihilation of Caste.*

We settled into the sofa. After tea and biscuits arrived we became more comfortable and relaxed. At 12.15 p.m. I suggested we could begin recording. This went on till 10.36 p.m., with several breaks mostly determined by Ramchandra

Singh. Madhu Singh left around 3 p.m. All told, I recorded over four hours of conversation, I figured later. Here, you will bear witness to how even Ramchandra Singh's speech has a literary flavour. The conversations were in Hindi. Where Ramchandra-ji uses English words, I have indicated the English using italics.

Anand: *If you don't mind I will turn this recorder on as we speak.*

RS: But do you want to begin right away? Should we not have some chai and then talk more formally later?

A: *Oh, it's not like that. We'll keep talking of course, formally and informally, and then see what from these conversations can be used. I'm now familiar with certain aspects of your life…*

RS: You have read the book, right?

Madhu Singh: *Oh yes, in fact he has read it twice over. The second time just before arriving here.*

A: *Yes, and I was riveted by it, and I have many questions like I told you over the phone. Which is why we are here. Tell us how you came to write the jail diary and how it came to be published.*

Anand Swaroop Verma, who was then editor of *Shaan-e-Sahara*, read the manuscript and published it in twenty-two instalments over successive weekends. I had written three-fourths of the manuscript in jail and had it smuggled out. How I did it is a long story. I did add a few chapters at the behest of Anand Swaroop-ji. There's no exaggeration in what I tell about the jail. In fact, what actually happens is far worse.

A: *After your book was published in 1991, and before that when your jail diary was serialised in* Shaan-e-Sahara *in the mid-1980s, what kind of reception did it have? Were there reviews or debates you remember?*

Shaan-e-Sahara was a popular weekly, and it also had a good circulation and was a progressive platform. I got a lot of response from the people. The weekly series reached even those involved with the [naxal] movement in the remote and hilly areas of the state. Many letters were published in the newspaper too. I even heard that the literary magazine *Hans* published a comment on or review of the book, though I did not read it. I recall reading that the poet and critic Hansraj Rahbar wrote a comment on it someplace. Some *literary-minded* people and those associated with the movement spoke positively about it. I don't have any of this material with me now. I've not kept a record of all this. I do not have copies either of the issues of *Shaan-e-Sahara* in which my diary appeared, nor do I have a copy of the edition published in the journal *Samkaleen Dastavez* by Prashant Kumar.

A: *How did you manage to get the manuscript out of prison?*

This was in Fatehgarh Central Jail. There was a unit for making ropes with cotton, and I was assigned to work there. There were many divisions in this manufacturing unit. The pakka who was in charge of the unit was sympathetic to me. He was not ideologically inclined though. When the manuscript assumed some density, the pakka suggested we find a safe place for it. He hid the manuscript in such a place among files that even the jailor would not spot it. In the middle of this, one day a new jailor took over, owing to the routine transfers that happen. The new jailor was taking an exhaustive inventory of all the things in this unit. We were afraid the manuscript would be discovered. Before he approached the files and the desk, there was a lunch break. That's when my friend made sure the manuscript disappeared and did not land in the jailor's hands.

The next issue was getting these papers out of jail where they were clearly not safe. So I sent word to Shiv Kumar Mishra-ji [Party leader], saying I needed to get across some crucial papers. This must have been around 1979–80. When visitors came to meet them, the prisoners were allowed to carry an empty bag or satchel with them so they could collect some eatables like roasted gram, sweets and savouries. Often even the empty bags of the prisoners [used to collect the gifts] were searched—and they of course frisked the bags of the visitors.

There was one Purushottam Sharma of Kanpur, who later became a bank employee, who was sent to meet me. You may have heard of Gopal Sharma, who was a cricket player and played for UP (Uttar Pradesh). He was among the first cricketers from UP to rise to national fame. Purushottam was Gopal's brother, the elder one. He brought some reading material for me in his bag, and we cleverly managed to sneak out the manuscript. Thus the handwritten manuscript was safely kept… Now, what's the point of this conversation that you are recording? Tell me: is there something that needs to be written or added to before turning this into a book?

A: *I thought we would just come over and have a conversation with you and see what comes of it… whether I write an afterword essay or present it as such in an interview format… we will see as we go along. There's no definite plan we came with.*

Oh we could of course keep talking… the story of my life after prison… should that be added, you think?

A: *After reading about your life in jail, there are a few questions that asked themselves in my head, both as a reader and as a publisher: you have described here, evocatively and powerfully, the thirteen years that stood still for you. This stagnancy of time that's indicated in the Hindi title, and then its flow, which of course is another matter… Consider me a reader who is quite ignorant but curious and interested. Having been raised largely in Telangana myself, I did not even know that the ideology of naxalism was well anchored in a place like Unnao district in UP. So I wish to know how did Ramchandra Singh-ji get drawn to naxalism. What was his life like before—in this village? What happened after the prison term and so on. Tell us about Bangarmau.*

In Bangarmau you can find every caste in the spectrum from brahmin to the doms, burial ground workers. The other poor and backward communities like chamars, lodhs, ansari, etc also are found in our village. I was born into a community called arak. It is listed as backward. It is a very poor community. I have experienced bitter poverty during childhood. I mean, what *experience* would a child have—I'd say we learnt to deal with abject poverty. There was no consciousness as such, but there was certainly an awareness that awakened within me. This room and this place we are now sitting in, this built-up house, all this was an open yard. We lived in a hovel. We'd forage leaves from trees for the few cattle we had. Both in winters and summers we'd be seen running around almost shirtless, half-naked. As far as education and schooling go, both in our family or in this mohalla, our neighbourhood, there was hardly anything during my childhood. You see, on this street where people of my caste, the arak, live, and in the adjoining street where the Mohammedans live—in this entire area, I was perhaps the first person to wear a pant. [Chuckles.] And that pant, I must tell you, was made of discarded cloth which we'd buy from faraway Kanpur. From this qasbah, I was also the first to study up to Class 12. What I mean to say is despite such dire circumstances there was this urge to educate myself, which is why I persisted. The situation at home was not such where they'd regard education as important and encourage me. I had to be self-motivated. The primary school was nearby, but after clearing fifth grade, my enthusiasm grew—in this entire block, I had come first. It felt good. I realised I had an aptitude. I continued till eighth grade in this region. That was when I met Shiv Kumar Mishra and other comrades.

Tell us something about Shiv Kumar Mishra. Where was he from, who was he…

He has his own history. During his student days, Mishra

[b.1916] became a member of the socialist party [Hindustan Socialist Republican Association] that had been founded [in 1928] by the pre-independence revolutionary leader, Chandra Shekhar Azad. Mishra participated in several militant struggles. After India gained political independence, he worked amongst the people based out of Kanpur, and his political work brought him to Unnao. He was a popular leader in this region. Mishra came under the patronage of Bishambar Dayal Tripathi [1899–1959] who was a leader of peasants within the Congress party, and who came under Subhash Chandra Bose's influence as well. He was born right here, in Bangarmau. Tripathi was in fact part of the Constituent Assembly and was elected to the Lok Sabha. Under Tripathi's guidance, Mishra formed the Communist Party here in 1937. The party became popular and its presence was felt in the entire district. Three of the party's candidates became legislators back then. The lives and histories of the leaders of those times and what we see now are of course vastly different. Shiv Kumar Mishra was such a man that even his opponents of the Congress considered him a magician of sorts. Mishra lived most of his life in Kanpur and led the Uttar Pradesh State Committee of the Communist Party of India (Marxist) and was a member of its Central Committee at the time of the naxalite movement. There was another well-known communist and labour leader, Comrade Ram Asrey.

Yes, he's mentioned in the book.

The one in the book, the youth leader Ram Asrey

Verma, is different. Comrade Ram Asrey of Kanpur, who was in the party politburo at one time, once wrote an essay in which he said Shiv Kumar Mishra was like *paaras patthar*—the philosopher's stone. Whatever he touched turned into gold. The point was that he was very charismatic and easily attracted the youth. I came in touch with the party then—it was still the undivided Communist Party. I attended daily workshops and meetings. People came to regard me as the 'party bachcha', the party boy. I may have been about fourteen then.

After eighth grade I left for Kanpur to continue [my education]. My aunt lived there in Coolie Bazar. I stayed with her. And I had to go all the way to Pandav Nagar to attend school, about eight to nine kilometres away. I'd often turn up late to school. Sometimes an hour late. The daily up–down was tough. Mostly by foot, but on the few days when I had some spare change I'd ride a bus. I started there in the ninth grade. The principal was an a imposing personality. He was making his usual rounds of the school grounds. All the children were in their classrooms. He held a huge black ruler in hand. I tried sneaking in quietly. He spotted me. And he summoned me. I think it was a sunny winter morning. He gave me one tight slap. I was stunned. He likely had no idea how I managed to make it to school—where I came from, how I managed to get my clothes, pay my fees, and the kind of hurdles on my path to education, all this flashed in my mind. Why does he get late? How hungry and thirsty does this boy go every day? All this context did not interest him. His job was to slap me. After he struck me and walked away, I just stood there. It was not as if he had hit me so hard that it hurt badly or that I was mentally traumatised. I can't say why I stood my ground. After a while, the principal turned back to look. For a moment, he hesitated. And he, in his heavy voice, summoned me again: Come here. You are still here? I blinked rapidly. What's your name? I told him. Where do you come from? I told him. From Coolie Bazar, on foot. He realised what this meant. Okay go now, try and reach on time from now.

About when was this?

[A long pause.] This must have been 1962. I remember because the Indo–China war was on. The Communist Party then was still undivided, but there was a great debate going on about whether or not to consider communist China an aggressor. At this point Shiv Kumar Mishra took [what later became] the CPI-M [Communist Party of India–Marxist] line. I was deeply under his influence. And he got arrested. He was put in the Unnao jail. All over the country, the CPI-M people were being jailed. I wrote a letter to him. I sent it from my school address. The CB-CID looked into this and made inquiries about where the letter had come from. In a month or so, a CID official turned up at our school. He told the principal that he was from the police intelligence wing and that he had to meet the student who wrote this. The school peon came to fetch me from my classroom. When I arrived, the principal did not know even my name…

Well, in a school of a thousand children how would he… but you remember the principal's name?

Yes, I do. Anyway, he quickly realised I was the same boy he had slapped. That picture must have stayed with him. He enquired about my class and section, and I told him. The CID man was seated there. The principal told me to take a seat. I stood still. When a principal asks you take a seat in front of him, any student would hesitate. So I kept standing. When he told me again to sit, I sat with trepidation. He asked if I knew the stranger seated next to me. When I admitted my ignorance, the principal explained the situation and told me the policeman would like to talk to me. I was asked if I knew Shiv Kumar Mishra. I said, Yes indeed. How? I said he was a well-known and highly regarded leader from my district. Where is he now? He's now been put in jail. The policeman's onus was to prove that I did write the letter. And this was easy to establish since I admitted to it. And then he left.

What did you write in the letter?

It was not much. Back then I did not understand ideology or the debates about China and what line to take. I was just overcome by emotion when a beloved leader like Mishra was incarcerated. He was such a good man, and I felt bad about what had befallen him. It was not as if the contents of the letter were explosive from any point of view. For the police, it was enough that such a letter was written. It was [grounds for] a routine query.

Around this time, I think in 1963, when I was in inter college, in my eleventh grade I think, the great scholar Rahul Sankrityayan died. By then, I had formed a group of like-minded school friends, and we discussed political, social and literary matters. In that circle, I made some very good personal friends too: Mukti Kumar Mishra was one, and Artiman Tripathi was another. There was also Shiv Sagar Tripathi. These were politically conscious youngsters. Our group resolved to organise a condolence meeting. We went to the principal and said since Rahul Sankrityayan had passed away they must call for a condolence meeting, declare a holiday and close the school for the day as a gesture of respect. It was not as if we had expected the principal to immediately respond to our demand. It was more to convey to him that we were aware of the world of letters outside of the school. Some kind of posturing was also involved, you could say. In the letter we had drafted we spoke about how the great litterateur, scholar and thinker Sankrityayan had died and why we needed a discussion of his legacy.

Right above the principal's office the school manager had a room where he lived. We consulted him and showed him our letter, asking him to forward it to the principal. In an hour or so, the peon came to each classroom informing the teachers that classes were being suspended for the day and that we were all to assemble in the ground. When this notice reached our class, we jumped with joy. We realised that it was based on our application that the action had been taken.

Everyone was now gathered at the ground. Chairs had been arranged. The principal, the manager and other important school functionaries were seated there. It was not as if I or anyone in my circle knew much about Rahul Sankrityayan other than that he was a reputed writer, and that he had some revolutionary ideas. We had read an essay or two by him at best. We were no experts. It was the principal who spoke first. He was impressed that we had been aware of the significance of someone like Rahul Sankrityayan and that we wanted to remember him. Then he spoke about the legacy of Sankrityayan. Soon, he asked me to come on stage to speak. I don't recall what I said but I did speak without fear or hesitation about how he'd espoused communism and stood up for socialist ideals. The principal, who was of a nationalist persuasion, spoke a little and what followed is worth recalling. He had said that only time would tell whether socialism or the kind of liberal democracy we had was good for society. But when my friend Mukti Kumar Mishra got his turn to speak, he said: What say will the time to come have? We are the ones who determine the time to come. I thought: would there be a fight now... [chortles] but principal sir too broke into a laugh.

This was how school was. My emotional *interaction* with and closeness to the principal thus kept increasing.

Would you mind telling us the principal's name...

Yes of course. I will tell you his name, about the house he lived in... [chuckles]

And the name of the school, was it a government school or private…

It was an aided college. Well, GS Inter College is very famous in Kanpur. Ganesh Shankar Vidyarthi Inter College...

Madhu Singh: *Ganesh Shankar Vidyarthi was a nationalist, something of a revolutionary, a well-known Gandhian and founder-editor of the Hindi newspaper* Pratap.

You know, Bhagat Singh, when he was on the run, took refuge at the *Pratap* office… he did his reading and writing and even lived there. Vidyarthi supported Bhagat Singh, Chandra Shekhar Azad and other revolutionaries, and they used to write both in their own name and pseudonymously for the paper. We have digressed. To come back to the college and the principal… In those days, first division was a rarity. I did not get a first division in my high school. But within the school, I got the highest marks when I matriculated. For my teachers, this was a matter of great pride. It must of course have occurred to the principal: this boy comes all the way, the boy I slapped… You see the principal lived far closer to the school than I did. There was also a temple in that complex where he lived. The ground floor was a temple and the first floor had living quarters. It was a fairly large place. So he asked me to move in with him.

A: *If you had perhaps not stood a while and thought about the slap that day, and had he not turned back, all this may not have happened.*

MS: *It seems like a turning point.*

[Laughs loudly.] Soon after, he said you may find it difficult living and studying where you live, so stay with us. Idealists of this kind, such teachers, are rare. Actually he had a lot of property that came his way through his in-laws. He had a few tenants too. All this aside, he had humanist values. There was a spare room on the top floor where I was to live. They gave me atta, dal and other provisions. Often the principal's wife would call me out and offer what she had cooked. The point is we became *familiar* with each other.

I think the word familiar in Latin comes from family, indicating being close to the family.

Could be true. Their son was called Suman. He went on to become a doctor.

But you never took the principal's name.

The principal's name was Hiralal Shukla. Now let's have lunch.

If I may say so, it looks like in your life…

…there were a lot of brahmins [chortles].

[We break for lunch and a little while after this, around 3 pm, Madhu Singh heads back to Lucknow. Ramchandra Singh and I resume the conversation.]

A: *We were talking of the brahmins in your life: they seem to have been around you and you around them. Tiwari, Tripathi, Shukla, Mishra, Dwivedi, Pandey. Now, you said the principal believed in humanist values, but did it not matter to members of his family that you belonged to some other caste considered low?*

Of course people did think of caste. But his family were

generous. They used to support a lot of poor, backward, underprivileged students with their education. I stayed with them for a year or so I think. I did not immediately finish my twelfth. There was a gap of a year or two. Let me tell you a story that will give you an idea of the principal's *character.* During the time I lived with them, there was a statewide teachers' strike. They had a set of demands. To discuss the demands of the teachers, all the principals of Kanpur had a meeting. A principal of course earns better and belongs to a different class, and often has views that reflect that class. Most of the principals were unanimous in saying that the teachers were wrong and did not deserve support. But our principal, Hiralal Shukla, took a different view. He opposed their resolution and supported the teachers. His argument was that we are teachers first, principals next. He also felt the demands of the teachers were just. Some of the principals were on state boards and committees and benefitted from this. For strategic and selfish reasons they did not want to antagonise the state and hence were against the strike. They feared that if they supported the strike they may not be able to remain on or get onto some board or committee and so on. But our principal did not buy into this. In the next few days he was at the forefront of the teachers' strike and went to jail. It was a matter of four or five days but he did this on a point of principle. Now you can see what kind of a man he was.

A: *Did you ever meet him after you got out of jail?*

No, I could not. He had died by then. After I got arrested

he wrote me a letter. He said he was not keeping well, and if he got better he would pay me a visit in prison. He did not manage to visit. After I got out, I asked around and found that he had passed away. I've huge respect for him, but in the end I'm sad I did not get to see him again. Memories are all I have… I did meet his son, Ravindranath Suman, who was a doctor. When this jail diary was published, he subscribed to *Shaan-e-Sahara*, and he read my story. There was one Kamlesh Tripathi, a journalist who worked for *Shaan-e-Sahara*. Suman was acquainted with him. So it seems Suman asked Kamlesh if this Ramchandra Singh was not the same fellow from Bangarmau. That was when I went to meet Suman.

The book begins with your being tortured and rivulets of blood trickling down your face. Tell us what landed you in prison and about your association with the naxal movement.

In 1967, the outbreak in Naxalbari happened. I joined the students movement in Kanpur. I became active in the Unnao district unit of CPI-M. Back then a proper naxalite party had not emerged and we still stuck around with CPI-M despite debates and differences. At a very young age, I became a member of the party's district committee. I used to attend meetings. It was then that Charu Mazumdar gave the slogan of returning to the villages. The call was for educated students to move from cities to villages and prepare and mobilise the people towards a revolution. All over the country, young men and women responded to this call. But what village would I go to? I was from a village. It was then decided that I'd go to Bahraich, the northern district that borders Nepal. I went to the qasbah of Nanpara under the guise of continuing my education. It was there, while working in the naxalite movement, that I appeared for my intermediate exams from Prayagpur.

Meanwhile, in Unnao the situation was becoming conducive for revolution. So I returned here and resumed party work. Around this time I even took admission to BA in Kanpur. In Unnao those days the slogan was for annihilation. Charu Mazumdar called for a campaign to *annihilate class enemies.* In this context preparations were underway and I contributed to them. This is when I too participated. The police in Unnao was after us, so we moved to the neighbouring Hardoi district. There's a village there called Bakhaura, about fifteen kilometres from Bangarmau where we are now. It is on the Unnao–Hardoi border. There was a terrible landlord there. We *annihilated* him. We used to target the zamindars who terrorised the workers. It was in the Bakhaura case that I was arrested. That led me to jail.

How come you did not escape and got arrested?

Some of us escaped after committing the annihilation and some of us were apprehended on the spot. I'll explain why and how. About ten to twelve of us went to that village. We split into two groups. One went into the house of the landlord and another kept vigil outside. The group that went in killed the man. We heard gunfire. Our implements were small pistols and crude bottle-bombs. There was commotion in the village and the villagers chased us. The question that arose—and we reflected on this only later, after we landed in jail—was this. In a place where we had not worked to create a *social base*, where we had not worked enough among the common people to understand and reflect upon their local concerns and issues, this is what happens. The villagers we thought we were helping by annihilating an oppressor-landlord, these very people ran after us and nabbed us. And handed us over to the Mallawan police. If we had worked towards creating a *base* and awakened the people, things may have been different. It was not as if we had not anticipated such a turn of events. A few of us did raise this issue with the Party before the *action*. But then we were mocked. You are scared, we were told. I said I was not afraid and would go along with what the majority decided. But I did present my view. What I felt was that by murdering individuals we were not going to effect a revolution. Mobilising the *masses* was not done. I landed in jail but such incidents kept happening as part of the naxal upsurge.

How old were you? In the book you say your moustache was still nonexistent when you landed in jail.

I must have been twenty or twenty-one. And in the jail they'd ask one question and before you answered it, they'd ask another. That was to disorient you. But at the outset I told them, I know everything you wish to know from me [about the organisation]—though in fact I did not know everything—but I will tell you nothing. And since I won't tell you anything, you might as well subject me to *torture* straightaway. Do not waste your time, and start. It is a psychological game, you see.

Over thirteen years, you were moved across five jails. Where did you spend the longest time?

In Fatehgarh Central jail. Then I was shifted to Lucknow jail and lastly to Faizabad. Which is where I was shifted to a *superior class* during my last few months. Do you understand what *superior class* is?

No. You do mention towards the close of the book that this happened near the end of your term but you have not explained what it entailed.

This means a high class prisoner. You'd get special facilities—both in terms of living and eating. Let me tell you the history of this. During the British period, the *political prisoners* often staged strikes, went without food etc. They said they needed to be recognised as political prisoners and not be classed with other prisoners, who were looked down upon as ordinary criminals of a lower class. One young man, a Bengali, Jatin Das, an independence activist with the Congress was incarcerated in the Lahore jail in the 1920s. He staged a sixty-four-day hunger strike and then died in jail. After that, the British came to recognise political prisoners as a separate class. In the post-independence period this category became defunct. But instead of re-introducing the category political prisoners, the state allowed for something called *superior class*. And this meant that not just politicians or those espousing political causes like, say, naxalites, anyone could be placed in this category if they had the clout. Thugs and professional criminals would also get into this category. But this is a rare privilege. Earlier they even factored in the education of a prisoner and social status.

My political friend who used to work with us in the *field* and now practices in the Supreme Court in Delhi, Rakesh Dwivedi—he was in the Allahabad High Court when I was in jail. He filed a writ to get me superior class status.

Yes, he's mentioned in the book. If we are talking of the same person, I think I happen to know his daughter Divya Dwivedi, and I met her only recently, and this was after reading your book in manuscript form. Divya teaches at IIT-Delhi. And I even wondered if her father could be the same person you mention in the book but wasn't sure since Rakesh is in another league today...

He's now a top lawyer in Delhi and is at the Supreme Court. He belongs to a family of vakils. He represents high-profile politicians now—like Lalu Prasad Yadav in the fodder scam, Mulayam Yadav in the disproportionate assets case, Jayalalithaa and so on. He used to live in Noida, but now lives somewhere in Jor Bagh I heard. Rakesh used to work for the party, CPI-ML. We worked a lot together. You know his son is now a cricketer, called Ekalavya Dwivedi. His daughter was too young and may not remember me. I remember once she got herself a long Hanuman-like tail and used to run around the bungalow with it. She was a child, she may not remember me. This was when Rakesh was with the Allahabad High Court.

[Meanwhile, excited by this connection, I text my new-made friend Divya asking if she was free to talk.]

Are you in touch with Rakesh now? Would he have read your book?

We have fallen out of touch. I have no idea if he's read my book or not. When I went to Delhi sometime recently to invite people for my son Rishi's wedding, I tried visiting Rakesh in Noida but I was told he had shifted to Jor Bagh. When I was in jail, he was at a leadership level in CPI-ML, in the Chandra Pulla Reddy group. He was even involved with the publication of a party newspaper *Hiraval Dasta* [The vanguard], published from Allahabad. He was its editor.

[My phone rings. It is Divya calling from Delhi. With Ramchandra-ji's permission, I take the call. I explain to her who I am with and where, and she's excited. I tell her about the tail she used to prance around the bungalow with in Allahabad. She tells me her dad has mentioned Ramchandra-ji and she would love to know more about what I am doing with him and what this book was about. I tell her the backstory briefly. After I hang up, I explain to Ramchandra-ji what the call was about. He is excited too, and says...]

...oh Divya. So we indeed have a proper *connection* now. What a coincidence. You know, Rakesh was involved with my informal wedding to my present wife, Vimala Devi. I was quite old by the time I was released and we just had a small informal function and it was Rakesh who solemnised it. [He calls out to his wife and tells her, Anand knows Rakesh's daughter. Vimala Devi tells me Rakesh is a well-wisher of the family. She then heads back into the recesses of the house.]

You say in the book how you were distressed on discovering Ramdulari the way you did in Delhi, living as someone's mistress. This is a question Madhu-ji the translator also had wanted to ask you... What happened after, and how did you end up marrying your present wife?

[Shifting to English] Oh please... [chuckles]... don't mind, don't take the name of that...

Oh, I'm sorry.

No-no. I will tell you that *portion* later. I feel...

You did not really formalise a marriage with her [Ramdulari] either is the sense I got from the book. It was just that she deemed you her partner, in love...

[Shifting to English] *After release, once or twice, she met me.*

Before your release she waits for you. She almost regards you her husband though there was no ritual of marriage.

You are right. There was no marriage.

She too was the daughter of a young widow, and to do all this at that time in a society where the mores were conservative must not have been easy.

You are right. Ours was an extreme case. Let's stop now and have dinner.

[While dinner is served, chicken and dal with rice and roti, the recorder is left on—intentionally or not I cannot now recall. Some excerpts.]

If you intend to add to or expand this jail diary—how do we go about it? Will I have to write something by myself, or will you pull something out of these conversations?

There are two ways of going about it, I was thinking. The first point is, it is your right to decide how this story gets to the world.

No it's not a question of authority…

Let me explain… I have spoken to you over several hours now. I have recorded a lot of this. Keeping this as a base, I will transcribe all that I can. You have a way with words—whether you are speaking or writing. You know how to build a narrative. So it could flow like we have conversed now, I think. Or I could turn this into an afterword essay about you, my trip etc. I'll get a better sense when I listen to all of this again, quietly. And then I will send you the transcript or whatever I manage to write. You will then read it. Make corrections where needed. If the English version is alright, you may read it in English or we could ask Madhu-ji to render this in Hindi, which may take time…

Oh no, I'd be happy to read it in English.

Then it's easy. And Madhu-ji could write a short essay or translator's note where she could tell us how she came across this text, how it affected her, why she felt compelled to translate it, how she met you and so on. We will open the book with "Thehre hue terah saal". The reader could start there and move on to these other narratives.

This sounds like a good plan.

My intention is to take this to as many languages as possible, from Telugu to French. That may or may not happen. It's just that I want as many readers for this as possible. After I read the translated manuscript, I told Madhu-ji I shall get on a train and visit you at the earliest.

[Conversation resumed after dinner.]

We were actually talking about Rakesh-ji getting you an upgrade in the prison.

Yes, it was Rakesh who filed a writ seeking to upgrade me to superior class. That is how an order came to be issued making me a superior class prisoner. There was a special barrack or facility for superior class prisoners in the Faizabad jail. All the superior class prisoners of the state were lodged here, and that is why I was shifted from Fatehgarh to Faizabad. This happened toward the very end of my term in jail.

The narrative in the book ends with barely a mention of this last phase of your life in prison which lasted about eight months. Tell me what were the special facilities extended here that you did not get elsewhere.

The bedding facilities were better. We got mosquito nets, cleaner linen. Even the headcount of prisoners was not done in a humiliating fashion like it happens in other barracks. They counted you right where you were stationed. The real important difference was in the rations we got. We were given both *veg* and *non veg*. In *non veg* you got 60 grams dal, 60 grams ghee, a quarter kilo of mutton, a portion of rice, wheat flour, turmeric, spices, milk, tea and so on. Everything was itemised. All this was procured and prepared by the kachcha. A soap to bathe, towel, toothpaste, one newspaper, a weekly magazine, etc were assigned too.

What role did a rookie prisoner (kachcha) have here?

Every superior class prisoner was provided with a helper. In jail language he was called a *safaiyya*—the one who cleans up and attends to all your needs. This person was from among the newbies at the prison. It was not written down that only a newbie be assigned but that had come to be the custom.

So a personal slave of sorts was attached to a superior class prisoner? Sounds like some kind of gulamgiri.

Yes, you could say that. It was gulamgiri. Every morning at the assigned hour before breakfast, the safaiyya would turn up here from his barrack. All the safaiyyas would go fetch the provisions for the day, including the wood and coal required to cook. Even vessels—pans, plates, glasses and so on—were assigned separately. Within the superior class cell, there was a cabin meant for cooking. The poor safaiyya also had to wash the clothes of the privileged prisoner. He was around us from sunrise to sunset—from the jail's opening till its closing. And the timings varied according to the season.

Do you remember the name of the safaiyya who served you?

You see there used to be a clamour among safaiyyas who would ask the warders to be assigned to me.

This was because you were nice to them?

Must have been the case. You see most of the superior class prisoners had *feudal* mindsets. A few of them were even mahant types from Ayodhya during my time there. These bastards used to get the safaiyyas to press their feet and get massages done. Now, regarding *non veg*, it was in the evening that these rations were to be collected from the store. And the safaiyya would then cook it the way the senior prisoner wanted it. Let me tell you about how people found ways to make money on the side with this system. Sometimes the prisoner would decide he'd not have *non veg* on certain days. But it would be still marked in the relevant ledgers that he'd been assigned the meat. The large share of the money thus saved from these portions of meat would then be paid in cash to the prisoner. The safaiyya colluded in this. In this manner, a superior class prisoner could make anything between two hundred to five hundred rupees a month in those times. Using this, sometimes when you'd get tired of chicken or mutton, you could get them to procure some fish with the spare money.

Did the safaiyya get to eat some of the good stuff he cooked?

There was nothing written down about his getting this food but I used to share some of it with the safaiyya assigned to me. Say, we were assigned four eggs. I'd ask my safaiyya to make two separate double-egg omelets: one for him and one for me. As per the rules, the safaiyya would have to go his barracks and fetch his allotted cooked meals. But I'd let him share the food he made for me. Naturally the dal and vegetables served in the other barracks were of inferior quality. So the safaiyyas assigned to me were always happy.

Do you remember the name of any of the safaiyyas who served you?

[Pauses and thinks.] There was some Pandey. Wait, it will

come back to me… I remember another safaiyya though, Munshilal. He belonged to a village by the Sarayu river near Ayodhya. He was mallah by caste. During my time in the Faizabad jail, he had returned to the prison after a gap of some years. He served me as safaiyya on a few occasions. The local police frequently hauled up young men from their neighbourhood and put them in jail for petty crimes. Munshilal was among them. He would often talk to me about his home, family, community and his background. There was another safaiyya, whose name I now forget. He landed in jail for picking pockets. With his rather honest and straightforward looks, he did not appear to be a pickpocket to me. I thought he was innocent and must have been framed. One winter day, I was sunning myself, sitting on a slope. He came and sat by my side. When I told him how I thought he was innocent, he said, 'Well, in this matter I'm indeed innocent. Poverty and the bad company I kept pushed me towards this.' When I asked how pockets are picked, he smiled and refused to show how it's done. Then we chatted about many things. When the patch of sun moved away, he stood up to leave. 'Sir, here, take this.' He opened his fist and handed me a two-rupee note. 'This note is yours,' he said. I quickly checked my pocket and the two-rupee note I had there was missing. 'When you were busy talking to me, I picked your pocket to show how it is done.' I was surprised but not angry with him.

You see there were some feudal lords during my time

there. There was this man said to be the chief of the Akhil Bharatiya Kushti Mahasangh [Wrestling Federation of India]—Brij Bhushan Sharan Singh. After he got out of prison, he went on to become a Member of Parliament with the Bharatiya Janata Party and then joined the Samajwadi Party. He would throw his weight around but was otherwise an alright man. He interacted very little with the safaiyya. He kept his distance... We were assigned dhoti and towels, and during winters, we got a coat and warm clothes too. All this came from the Khadi Bhandar. When I was to be released just as winter set in, I decided to keep my warm clothes and coat. The deputy jailor in charge of the stores said but this is jail property. Of course I knew that, but I told him if he let me out in the cold now, how would I manage? So they let me be.

What was the first thing you did on release? Did anyone come to receive you?

No one did. The first thing I did was I went to see my mother. She lived in Kanpur. That is where the book ends. Then I went hither and yon. Like a leaf that falls off the pipal tree floats without a sense of direction or purpose.

Like Kabir is believed to have said: Patta toota dal se, legayi pavan udaay, ab ke bichdha na miley, dur pade hai jaay. The leaf leaves the tree, the wind renders it free.

Life was of course its own purpose. But you see the party now had so many groups. There was Kanu Sanyal airing his own views, the CPR group pulling another way. But the thought I had was that when I returned from jail the comrades would welcome me, and I could do some new work with them… that did not happen for a while.

Where were all the comrades?

They had all scattered. Some had settled down into a middle-class life. I did eventually meet up with members of the Chandra Pulla Reddy group. Shiv Kumar Sharma was in the CPR group; there was one Harbhajan Singh of Punjab working in this area. Rakesh Dwivedi was in this circle though I did not meet him immediately. Then we took this *line*—of organising the masses on important issues. One issue we took up was in a place called Raiwala near Haridwar in the terai region. There, a seth called Panjvani had occupied 900 acres of village land. He had built a Maa Anandamayi ashram there. He had colluded with government officials and seized the land. The main leaders of this movement to reclaim the land were Shiv Kumar Sharma, Rakesh Dwivedi and Bhagwant Singh. This became famous as the Doon Ghati Sangharsh. After that in Allahabad, Rakesh did some good work organising agricultural labourers against landlords. Even in Hardoi district we worked among the masses. I was involved with all this. Bhumihin Kisan Sangharsh Samiti [Forum for Landless Agricultural Workers] was also formed by the CPR group. Its first congress happened right here, in Bangarmau. Rakesh Dwivedi was elected head of the regional committee and I was on the committee too. At least six to seven thousand delegates attended. A lot of dalit and Backward Caste women from many districts were there too.

You see, my present wife, she too attended the conference. She and a lot of local women ran the kitchen for the conference… Now tell me, is this bed comfortable for you to sleep in?

Oh yes, I am most comfortably settled.

It reminds me of a saying we have: Neend na jaane tooti khaat.

Hmm. Sleep doesn't care for a broken cot. This must have emerged from among the working classes. Is there more to this?

Ishq na jaane jaat-kujaat. Bhookh na jaane jhootha bhaat. And you can keep adding to it.

Love doesn't care for caste-subcaste. Hunger does not spurn leftovers.

And where were we?

You were speaking of how the Doon Ghati Andolan...

Yes, there was then the Bara–Karchana movement near Allahabad against feudal high-handedness, the rights of agricultural workers. Rakesh was at the helm of it. The Party's organisational aspects were getting strengthened. I had a role in it. I was a state committee member of the Party. In Bareilly, the Party managed to make an office, and I was assigned to work there. Meanwhile, my wife stayed with the joint family in Bangarmau, where my father and brother were. My father was supportive and we somehow managed. The newspaper that Rakesh Dwivedi used to edit, *Hiraval Dasta*... first it used to be published from Allahabad. It was briefly stopped, and we revived it from the Bareilly office. And the state committee made me its editor for about two years. This was around the time, 1984 I think, when my jail diary was serialised in *Shaan-e-Sahara*. Once I settled into this routine, I took my wife along as well. We stayed over a year in Bareilly. It was then decided that a party office be started in Pilibhit so that we worked in the rural interior. The state secretary, Harbhajan Singh, alias Jaswant—he had a place there. So I was moved to the Pilibhit office. In the midst of all this, I noticed a bad tendency had come to afflict and spread in the Party. The leadership was becoming increasingly self-centred. People began to think of their own personal gains. Jaswant too became a victim of this tendency.

How exactly did they turn selfish? Did they give too much importance to their own lives?

Exactly. Their personal lives assumed priority. And this happens when we lose faith in the revolution or even social change. When we think nothing's going to change. In Pilibhit, I worked in rather difficult circumstances. In those days Pilibhit was called 'mini Punjab'. There was a lot of terrorist activity—the Khalistan movement. The communists were also their target. I'm using the word terrorist here because they demanded the creation of a state, a nation, on the basis of religion. Large sections of Punjabis too opposed this of course. Among these opponents were many communist leaders who were targeted and killed. Many of the CPI-ML's CPR group leaders were also attacked—Baldev Singh Mann, later Sarabjit, Jaimal Singh Padda were among those killed. Back then, Baldev Singh Mann's letter to his daughter became very famous. Have you read or heard of it?

No I have not. Tell me.

He was in his village, called Bagga Kala in Amritsar. His in-laws lived, if memory serves, in Sitapur village of Pilibhit district. His wife lived there and she gave birth to a daughter. When Mann got the news, he drafted her a letter. He was to post it. He had kept it in his pocket, and was about to post it or something. But then got killed by the Khalistani forces. This was in 1986 I think. Later, the police found the letter in his shirt pocket. The letter got published and it became very popular across the world. These were the circumstances in which we worked in Pilibhit... then we returned, and I began to work for the Party right here in Bangarmau. There was a terrible landlord in this region called Mahavir Singh, a thakur, who tormented the dalits and the poor. It was feudal terror. The man even kept an elephant. There was one man of the paasi community called Hira, and another of the chamar community called Thakuri. Their grandfathers had borrowed grain some twenty-three years ago from the landlord. The dalits could never repay the debt. Hira and Thakuri would set out for Mahavir's fields and slog all day for the landlord. For free. It was *begar*, bonded labour. We took up this issue and freed the bonded labourers. Mahavir Singh said even if Hira and Thakuri died he would get *sira* done on their bodies—that is smear them with liquid jaggery—and get his dogs to lick them. But we managed to get Hira and Thakuri out of his clutches. How we did that is a long story. Now let us go to bed. What time do you normally wake up?

Usually around 6 a.m. When should we start for Lucknow tomorrow?

We will start by about 9 or so. We can talk in the car if it's alright. Would it be possible to record in the car?

Yes, should be, if we raise the windows.

[It is 10.36 p.m. and we both turn in. The recordings made the next day in the taxi ride back were not clear.]

The many lives of a memoir

Translator's afterword

Madhu Singh

I first chanced upon Ramchandra Singh's diary *Thehre Hue Terah Saal* (1970–83) in 2012 at Dastavez Prakashan in Lucknow, is a treasure house of books and a favourite haunt of scholars, researchers and students alike. Singh's diary was published in *Samkaleen Dastavez* [Contemporary Dossier], a short-lived Hindi literary journal. The pages of the journal had yellowed and turned brittle by the time I laid my hands on them. The slim monthly, in a landscape format with stapled pages, bore the colophon: Issue 2, Year 1, May 1991. Below the masthead came the address: 3/29 Patrakar Puram [Journalists Enclave], Gomti Nagar, Lucknow, 226001, phone 391610. The editor of the journal was Prashant Kumar, who had been a journalist.

Samkaleen Dastavez first arrived on the scene in April 1991 with the issue titled "Angarey" (Embers) featuring the transliteration into Devnagari script (by Shakeel Siddiqui) of the eponymous and controversial 1932 Urdu language collection of nine short stories and a one-act play, edited by Sajjad Zaheer with contributions from Ahmed Ali, Mahmuduzzafar, Rashid Jahan and others. The first *Angarey*, the product of the Progressive Writers' Movement founded in London, was banned by the colonial British government in 1933 at the behest of the All-India Shia Conference.

In his inaugural editorial, Prashant Kumar dwelt upon the rise and decline of "alternative journalism" aimed at social change and emphasised the need for "little magazines" in Hindi such as *Uttargatha* (Mathura), *Vartman Sahitya* (Ghaziabad), *Samkaleen Janmat* (Patna). The journal was acutely aware of the difficult road ahead:

Samkaleen Dastavez may continue to be published or may even close down after a few issues. But we have been preparing ourselves for this struggle for years together and will try our best to take it forward. We will reach you every month with a meaningful dossier. Each issue will be a special issue. We will put complex truths before you in simple language and style—also through investigative reporting, essays, statistics, stories, poems, images and cartoons. We will break old and new myths with new and old dossiers. We shall look forward to you always for your writings, suggestions, and support.

The third issue, guest-edited by the critic Virendra Yadav, was called "Partition Jaari Hai"— Partition in Progress—a collection of ten stories that "explored Hindu–Muslim relations and various aspects of communalism". It featured the work of renowned writers such as Shrilal Shukla, Amarkant, Gulsher Khan Shaani, Abdul Bismillah, Manzoor Ehtesham, Habib Kaifi and Muhammad Tahir among others, with cover art by the American artist Paul Davis (whose work has featured in *Rolling Stone* and *The New Yorker*). Financially unviable, *Samkaleen Dastavez* shut shop after five issues, and Dastavez Prakashan was founded in the early 1970s where back issues of the defunct journal can still be found.

That *Samkaleen Dastavez* devoted its entire second issue to Ramchandra Singh's jail diary, featuring illustrations credited to Om Jhingran, speaks volumes of the regard this work had come to assume. The editorial said that the jail diary was a revised and edited version of the serialised story of the naxal prisoner first published in *Shaan-e-Sahara*, a Hindi weekly from Lucknow. Prashant Kumar underscored the need to republish the diary: "Not many authentic accounts of prison and prison conditions were available. In India, celebrity political leaders who penned their prison memoirs were generally unaware of the great rot and corruption in prisons. Also, they mostly wrote about themselves or about party politics." He observed that "rarely do we come across such records which inform the society about the struggles and sufferings of common prisoners and undertrials in confinement ..." Moreover, "not much attempt has been made in Hindi journalism or literature to throw light on the oppressive prison system."

Such an account kindled my interest. Its setting, a region of Uttar Pradesh with a little-known connection to the naxalite insurgency, was intriguing. My in-laws also came from an area not far from the scene of action in the book and belonged to the class Singh and his comrades meant to 'annihilate'. When Singh was incarcerated in 1970, I was far removed from his world—a gangly middle-class girl with a pair of ponytails fastened with 'Love-in-Tokyo' rubber bands, studying in grade six at a local convent school. His narrative showed how the imposition of the Emergency in 1975, and the ruthless police repression that ensued, were directed against such little pockets of influence that the naxalites had secured across different parts of the country. Since Uttar Pradesh does not fall within what is termed the 'red corridor', Singh's diary seemed to me a crucial document in plugging a gap in the historiography of the naxalite movement in India.

As I read through the pages, what was apparent was his own ideological dilemma at a moment when the leadership of the Communist Party of India (Marxist–Leninist) was in crisis. He was influenced by his mentor, Comrade Shiv Kumar Mishra, who had opposed the Charu Mazumdar-directed 'annihilation' programme that swept the country after 1969; Kumar had written several essays to expose its hollowness.

During the thirteen years he spent across five jails of Uttar Pradesh, Ramchandra Singh realised that prison had become an outdated institution with a heavy colonial hangover; infested with oppression, corruption and malpractices of all kinds; an institution that benefited none—neither the society nor the prisoners and their families, not even the bureaucracy. No good could come of a system which destroyed people so thoroughly that they had little chance to recover or reform.

Besides the play of human emotions and the complex

nature of relationships forged in the confined space of prison, other features such as the 'panopticon' nature of a prison, the mechanisms and techniques employed towards constant surveillance, torture and isolation held my attention. It was indeed a gripping tale of oppression and power play—the inmates under a constant 'gaze', "a state of conscious and permanent visibility that assured the automatic functioning of power," as Foucault says in *Discipline and Punish: The Birth of the Prison*. Once the prison gates had slammed shut behind them, they existed in a sort of netherworld, invisible to people outside, while inside they were stripped of autonomy and deprived of any identity besides that of a convict, a criminal, an inmate. Most importantly, the diary-memoir came to terms with the past by reclaiming the self—in its continuity, its intellectual and moral agency—all the way through a prolonged experience of disruption, trauma and powerlessness. This was a vital step towards healing and also a much needed ethical act.

As I began translating, I often struggled to find suitable equivalents for terminology, context-specific terms and slogans, the nuanced social and political context in which the 'original' work functioned, and ideological issues and concerns I wasn't familiar with. A few phone calls to Ramchandra Singh and meetings with him, mostly at the Indian Coffee House in Lucknow, helped. The most striking thing when I first met him was the scar of a long gash on his face; I was immediately reminded of the opening lines of the book. He also had a limp. While the scar was the memento of his early days in prison, the limp owed to a recent road accident—but his spirit remained as doughty as ever. A gentle bespectacled man who thinks deeply before he speaks, Singh has a keen photographic memory and can retrieve past events and people in a matter of seconds.

Once the translation was ready, I looked for a publisher and the responses I received were not too encouraging. At an academic conference in the United States, I came to know about Navayana in New Delhi. Its publisher S. Anand readily agreed to publish it after reading the manuscript. Last published in 1991 in the little read *Samkaleen Dastavez*, Ramchandra Singh's diary had languished long enough in anonymity, awaiting a resurrection.

Following Anand's daylong interview with Ramchandra Singh in Bangarmau, I decided to meet Anand Swaroop Verma, who was a sub-editor at *Shaan-e-Sahara* in 1984. Verma was behind the serialisation of Singh's story, taking it to the Hindi public. I realised that without meeting him, my journey as a translator would not be complete. A prolific translator himself, as well as being a writer, critic and poet, he is currently the editor of the Hindi journal *Samkaleen Teesri Duniya* (translates as 'Contemporary Third World'). Before I could ask what inspired him to publish Singh's story, he was curious about why I chose to translate a naxal diary. I admitted that mine was an academic engagement with an important issue of our times. More important, I felt Ramchandra's story and the many stories it contains deserved a wider audience. Translation, for me, is a means of exploring new ground. This micro-narrative from the margins set itself apart from the widely reported meta-narrative of the Maoist struggle.

When I visited Anand Swaroop Verma's modest office in Noida, near Delhi, I was accompanied by Ramchandra Singh. To Verma's left was a row of rusting, open shelves stacked with an amazing range: books from Third World countries, particularly Africa; progressive, classic and contemporary literature in Hindi and English; translations from other languages from across the country and the world; bundles of old and new journals and magazines. In 1977, he had translated Mary Tyler's *My Years in an Indian Prison* into Hindi (*Bharatiya Jailon Mein Paanch Saal*). Tyler, a British citizen who had married a Bengali, spent five years as a 'naxalite' prisoner in the Hazaribagh jail in Bihar. Later, in Lucknow, when Verma met Ramchandra Singh who had just got out of prison, he suggested that Singh write a memoir. Singh had already kept a diary in various prisons and had managed to steal most of it out. The memoir he went on to reconstruct from these fragments turned out a valuable document, more powerful, informative and gripping than the offerings of convict celebrities and political leaders. The reception of the serialised story was just as remarkable. According to Verma:

As the chapters of the diary started coming in, I was certain that his work was actually very different from those I had read earlier. Ramchandra Singh had articulated the experiences and struggles of the prison most accurately... The readers' response was extremely encouraging ... they waited every week for the episodes to come out.

At Verma's office, I was lucky to find the first issue of the *Shaan-e-Sahara* dated 1 April 1984 and the subsequent issues which had carried the 'episodes'. The broadsheets of the weekly were yellow and fragile with age but the print was clear. The title given by Verma was "Umr qaid ke seenkhachon se: Ek naxalvadi ki jail diary" (Behind bars for life: The diary of a naxalite). The blurb announced the story to be "beyond imagination, adventurous, memorable", and it introduced the writer as someone who had suffered brutality in jail. It described the particularly trying circumstances in which the diary was secretly written by a 'C-class' prisoner, and how the chapters were smuggled out amid tight security.

Often when a translator tries to render a work into a new language, she flits in and out of the two languages and cultures, trying to do justice to the act. Like the scholar Marilyn Gaddis Rose says in her 1997 work *Translation and Literary Criticism Translation as Analysis*, as a translator I felt I "reside(d) not in one or another language or culture, but rather in an 'inter-liminal' area or middle ground, where any two languages intersect." Living in translation, I had a dual life.

Over the course of working on this, I realised that Ramchandra Singh's story, too, had acquired multiple lives of its own. It was thrice born—twice in Hindi, and now finally in English. The 1984 and 1991 versions of Ramchandra Singh's story survived the passage of time, on each occasion revised and updated, marked by helpful interventions by editor-publishers, to reach a new audience. In the present edition of the book, his life in prison has been recreated once again from Hindi to English with copious inputs freshly added to the narrative by the author, often in response to queries raised by the publisher.

Thirteen Years: A Naxalite's Prison Diary (1970–1983) now begins its search for a new readership, a wider audience, a new life. I'm happy to have played my part in it.

Ramchandra Singh (1949–2018), of Bangarmau village in Unnao district of Uttar Pradesh, was a member of the Communist Party of India (Marxist–Leninist) Red Star, and served on its Central Committee. He was part of the editorial board of *Red Star Monthly* (Hindi). He passed away when this book was in press.

Madhu Singh is a professor in the Department of English and Modern European Languages, University of Lucknow. She has previously translated the scholar G.N. Devy's work, *A Nomad Called Thief*, into Hindi as *Ghumantu Hain Chor Nahin*.